THE
Truth & Life
of Myth

An Essay In Essential Autobiography

ROBERT DUNCAN

THE SUMAC PRESS

Fremont, Michigan

In cooperation with SOMA Books

This book was first published in a limited edition by The House
of Books, Ltd. in 1968.

This volume is published in cooperation with SOMA Books.
(GEORGE QUASHA, EDITOR)

Library of Congress Catalogue Card Number: 73-183486

Standard Book Number: 912090-18-9

THE TRUTH & LIFE OF MYTH

An Essay in Essential Autobiography

μύζω (A) *To make the sound* μὺ μῦ *or* μυμῦ, *to murmur with closed lips, to mutter, moan* . . . (B) *to drink with closed lips, to suck in* . . .

LIDDELL & SCOTT, Greek-English Lexicon, 1897 ed.

Possibly the first *muthos* was simply the interjectional utterance *mū*; but it is easy to see how rapid the development would be from interjection to narrative. Each step in the ritual action is shadowed as it were by a fresh interjection, till the whole combines into a consecutive tale . . . the life-history of the plant or the animal to be magically affected; it is the plot of the δρώμενον, for, says Aristotle, in a most instructive definition,

by myth I mean the arrangement of the incidents.

JANE HARRISON, Themis.

If all reality is taken only as it is given in the immediate impression, if it is regarded as sufficiently certified by the power it exerts on the perceptive, affective, and active life, then a dead man indeed still "is", even though his outward form may have changed, even though his sensory-material existence may have been replaced by a disembodied shadow existence.

ERNST CASSIRER, The Philosophy of Symbolic Forms,
II: Mythical Thought.

In such cases myth is the truth of the fact, not fact the truth of the myth.

KATHLEEN RAINE, "On the Mythological," Defending
Ancient Springs.

THE TRUTH & LIFE
OF MYTH

MYTH is the story told of what cannot be told, as mystery is the scene revealed of what cannot be revealed, and the mystic gnosis the thing known that cannot be known. The myth-teller beside himself with the excitement of the dancers sucks in the inspiring breath and moans, muttering against his willful lips; for this is not a story of what he thinks or wishes life to be, it is the story that *comes to him* and forces his telling. Wherever life is true to what mythologically we know life to be, it becomes full of awe, awe-full. All the events, things and beings, of our life move then with the intent of a story revealing itself. When a man's life becomes totally so in-formed that every bird and leaf speaks to him and every happening has meaning, he is considered to be *psychotic*. The shaman and the inspired poet, who take the universe to be alive, are brothers germane of the mystic and the paranoiac. We at once seek a meaningful life and dread *psychosis*, "the principle of life."

The meaning and intent of what it is to be a man and, among men, to be a poet, I owe to the workings of myth in my spirit, both the increment of associations gathered in my continuing study of mythological lore and my own apprehen-

NOTE. This study originated in a paper presented at a Conference on the Myth in Religion and Poetry convened by the Church Society for College Work in October 1967 at the National Cathedral in Washington, D. C.

sion of what my life is at work there. The earliest stories heard, nursery rimes and animal tales from childhood, remain today alive in my apprehensions, for there is a ground of man's imaginations of what he is in which my own nature as a man is planted and grows. Before I could read, my parents, my grandmother, my older cousins, had relayed Greek, Hebrew, and Germanic myth, along with family lore of early pioneer days in the West. The shaping of every spiritual and psychic imagination has its ground in these things that I did not originate but that came to me as an inheritance of what I was, a gift of life meanings. Today I still love, even foolishly, the signs and wonders, felt presences or nearnesses of meaning, where we must follow, in trust, having no more sure a guarantee of our arrival than does the adventurer in fairy or hero tale. And deep things, for me, will always be, beyond sign and wonder, the persons and acts that belong to the primal demand of the truth of a story. We all have a sense of the difference between what the story demands and what the teller of the story or the listener might like the story to be. The story that has been altered to be likely or true to some belief or to be pleasing or to have some other special effect upon its audience strays from its Self. So too there is a Self that belongs to a Story that determines the sense of truth and life in my own daily living. The *psychosis* or principle of the soul-life is its belonging to the reality of what we know to be true to our story-sense. In the light of the mythological, events and persons can seem true or false to the true story of who I am.

I

FOR my parents, the truth of things was esoteric (locked inside) or occult (masked by) the apparent, and one needed a "lost" key in order to piece out the cryptogram of who wrote

Shakespeare or who created the universe and what his real message was. From the theosophy of the 1890s my maternal grandmother had passed from Spiritualism to become an elder in an Hermetic Brotherhood, similar to and contemporaneous with the Order of the Golden Dawn to which Yeats belonged. Not only stories and books, but dreams and life itself, were to be read in terms of contained and revealed messages, even as in our time works of art, dreams and daily life are read by devotees of psychoanalysis, or as the People of the Book—Jews, Christians and Moslems—have always read God's intent in the world, in history, and whatever written record. For theosophists, psychoanalysts, and the converts of revealed religions, the story is not primary but the meaning behind the story.

Truth was for my parents primordial and spiritually dangerous. The Gnosis, like Eden and the Original Creation Itself, had once been perfect and complete—a simple sentence—"good" as *Genesis* testifies. But Gnosis, Eden and Creation, the very Word, had been lost in a Fall from Grace that we know as *knowledge*. The sentence, no longer simple, grows apprehensive of a duplicity. It covers what it is about to say. It rationalizes. It qualifies itself. Noah becomes drunk and bewildered from the fruit of that vine and threatens to say forbidden things.

Modern science, my parents believed, would come upon secrets of Nature, as science had come before in Atlantis upon such secrets, and, spiritually arrogant and ignorant, intoxicated by knowledge, destroy America—the New Atlantis—in a series of holocausts, an end of Time in my life time that would come in fire-blast, as the end of Atlantean Time had come in earthquake and flood. Plato's myth of Atlantis in *The Republic* was not, for my parents, an illustration of his political thought, the fiction of a Utopian society or the picture of a Platonic sociology. They saw what he called myth as most truly *secret*

[9]

and *lost* history. It was as if the whole of Plato's philosophy existed like a plant to bear the seeds of certain teachings: the reincarnation of the soul, the nature of demiurgic powers, the memory of Atlantis. The word *idea* meant for Plato something *seen*, and my parents thought of Plato's myths as true not to some story-sense but to vision. Ancient tradition—that Critias had the story from Solon who in turn had been *shown* in initiation by the priests at Saïs—had its guarantee in clairvoyant vision. Not only had Solon seen but Plato had also, they believed, seen in trance. Just as the key dreams in Freud's *Interpretation of Dreams* are his own, so Plato's myths were not, they believed, fictions but revelations of his own experience.

In this considerably Platonized theosophy, the mythopoeic mind was at once revered and mistrusted. If it not have the imprimatur of priestly knowledge, the natural creative imagination of the story-teller was to be mistrusted. The myths of priests were true; the myths of poets were deceptively true. Here, too, my parents' religion was Platonic, for Plato is most concerned to tell us that poets will play the truth false. The only antidote to the fictions and illusions of Poetry, Plato argues in the tenth book of *The Republic*, is the knowledge of their true nature unmasked by philosophy. But the fullness of Plato's knowledge, in the mixture of his story-telling and vision, lies in his poet's experience of such fictions and illusions as the fabric of his own work. The philosopher speaking of poetic imitations, accusing Homer and Hesiod of not knowing the truth of what they work, is haunted by the shadow of his own life work, where so often the trouble of a poetry, a creative magic, moves behind the dialectic. The Dialogues of Plato are also stories, and the truth of a story is not rooted in wisdom but in the sense of the drama of life. Or of the Life of life. For this sense is critical not only of wisdom but of our daily life as well. *"This stage,"* Shakespeare says in my *Venice Poem,* *"is Truth—*

[10]

```
                    never in living
                    but here, here
                    all felt things are
                    permitted to speak.
```

Where Philosophy raised a dialectic, a debate, toward what it calls Truth; Poetry raised a theater, a drama of Truth. And Plato the Mage, Plato the Magician, would be as powerful a person of our history as Plato the Philosopher, for he had theatrical reality. In the very beginning of my vocation as a poet, as I came to read Plato in my late teens, I was to be troubled by the question of the truth of the mythopoeic; and today as I continue to be involved with the reading of Plato, not only myth but truth itself is disturbing, the actuality of time itself disturbed by the reality of what is happening.

But since the seventeenth century, since the madness—the divine madness—of the religious wars, men have boldly striven to put away as irrational not only the enthusiasms of contending churches but myth and revelation itself. Christian and Hebrew myth have come to be, in the minds of rationalizing priests and rabbis, a psychological poetry, and, while, on the one side, there is a deepening of the sense of personal mystery, on the other, there is a drive to clear away the mythopoeic, the areas of creative and fictional contamination, and to establish a text in the light of what modern man is reasonably convinced is the likely or likeable truth of things. In a time when only one vision—the vision of an atomic disaster and the end of the species—haunts the world, in religion as well as in science, men labor to exorcize all the old stories. The spiritual and political promise of the day is that nothing will happen. The theater now must be not the theater of the most true but the theater of the absurd.

"*Modern man*," Rudolf Bultmann in his manifesto, *New Testament and Mythology*, argues, "*is convinced that the mythical view of the world is obsolete."* In the sweeping enthusiasm and persuasion of his modernist existentialism, no other contemporary thought seems *"modern"* to him. He either is not aware that the mythical view of the world is taken to be a primary apprehension of reality by men like Cassirer in his *Philosophy of Symbolic Forms* or Lévi-Strauss in *Le Cru et le Cui,* where the mythopoeic is fundamental to the structuring of man's world, or he dismisses such men without argument from the category of "modern man". The myth has been taken as the key to man's psychic life by Freud and the psychoanalytic schools. In Malraux's great *Psychology of Art,* myth, not aesthetics, appears as the moving force, a myth of forms. Indeed, Bultmann's theological challenge arises from the dramatic crisis sensed by the Christian imagination fascinated by the overwhelming power of another mythic view of the world—the story of the evolution of living forms that takes hold with Darwin's vision of the nature of the species and the various myths of the origin and destiny of the universe that arise from contemporary physics. As the story told of stars and subatomic particles and the story told of living organisms continue to reorient our possible knowledge of what is, the poetic imagination faces the challenge of finding a structure that will be the complex story of all the stories felt to be true, a myth in which something like the variety of man's experience of what is real may be contained. Yet this theologian calls not for the deepening and extension of our reading of mythological thought but for the abandoning of the mythopoeic itself. The message of the New Testament becomes purely humanistic, cleared of those gnostic and fictional elements in which man's intuitions and imaginations of his relation to the cosmic myth are embodied.

My thought as a poet has grown in the ground of twentieth-century mythologists like Cassirer and Freud, found a key in Jane Harrison's definition of the dithyramb as "the song that makes Zeus leap or beget", and followed the mythopoeic weavings of Pound's *Cantos* in which "all ages are contemporaneous". My sense of the involution of any idea with a story or stories it belongs to, of a universe of contributing contingencies, is such that my sentences knot themselves to bear the import of associations.

The roots and depths of mature thought, its creative sources, lie in childhood or even "childish" things I have not put away but taken as enduring realities of my being. The adult world always moved in realms above and beyond our understanding in childhood. The seed of poetry itself sprang to life in the darkness of a ground of words heard and seen that were a congregation of sounds and figures previous to dictionary meanings. The child hears the heart of speech, the emotional and illustrative creation, what Freudian or Jungian calls the *content* of what is said. He lives in the color of things, "the sweet influence which melody and rhythm by nature have," Plato says of the poet's persuasion:

> Thus every sort of confusion is revealed within us; and this is that weakness of the human mind on which the art of conjuring and of deceiving by light and shadow and other ingenious devices imposes, having an effect upon us like magic.

Like the poet, the child dwells not in the literal meanings of words but in the spirit that moves behind them, in the passional reality of the outraging or insidiously rationalizing adult. He hears not what his parents mean to say but what that saying is telling about them.

In the world of saying and telling in which I first came into words, there is a primary trouble, a panic that can still come upon me where the word no longer protects, transforming the threat of an overwhelming knowledge into the power of an imagined reality, or abstracting from a shaking experience terms for rationalization, but exposes me the more. I seek in Poetry to go as deep into "the passionate and fitful temper," as Plato calls it, of the soul as the sense of relations and ratios can carry me. The myth or pattern of elements in the story is a melody of events in which the imprint of a knowledge—knowledge, here, in the sense of a thing undergone—enters the generative memory and the history of man takes on tenor. "Melody, *Mélodia* in Greek, is the intonation of the *melos*, which signifies a fragment, a part of a phrase," Stravinsky tells us in his *Poetics of Music*. Not only in the symphony, but in the telling of the story and in the composition of the poem, powerful impulses towards pattern emerge along lines of felt relationships and equilibrations having their immediate locus in each immediate event of the poem. In actual life, great patterns of joy and suffering sweep away whole structures of ideal behavior; Fate moves men to disaster. "He who listens to her," Plato says—he speaks here of Poetry—"fearing for the safety of the city which is within him, should be on his guard against her seductions and make our words [the words of philosophy] his law."

The mothering and fathering voices about me conveyed a realm of pleasure and pain that I was to seek not to dismiss but to deepen. And there was a world too of wishful phantasy and the lore of generations in myth established in the serious appreciations of the adults about me. These first powers in their most awful moments—my mother and father, and my grandmother, my mother's mother, who was an elder in the Brotherhood—speaking in hushed or deepened voices, or speaking in voices that were not their own, regarded myth as they regarded certain poems and pictures as speaking from the realm of lost or hidden truth. Certain stories, not only Greek myths but fairy tales, not only fairy tales but certain modern fictions—*The Ice Queen* by Hans Christian Andersen or *The Princess and Curdie* by George MacDonald—were *true*. "You wont understand now, but you will later." The story of Jesus and the three Kings, the story of Hercules and his labors and of Jason and the Fleece, were more real than daily events. Or, it seemed that, later, life itself would reveal a reality in daily events that would bring one to understand all the old stories. Ones own true lifetime was a story, where at last ones own true companions were of the order of Joseph and Jesus, of Tip in *The Land of Oz* and of Isis who gathered up the lost parts of her husband Osiris. Whatever part ones parents as teachers played, and whatever part ones enchantment in the charm of the story-telling played, the stories, the music, the pictures that belonged to ones own life story seemed at once to be recognized and to recognize. "Thus every sort of confusion is revealed within us," Plato warns. And to speak at all of the operation of design, I would bring back the fullness of that warning. The city that is within us haunts all of Poetry. In *Heavenly City, Earthly City*, seeking to address the actual city of San Francisco, my own immediate city, I found myself in an other, "the darkened city of my perishable age." Reason and the ideal are futile indeed if they have not admitted the full range of our human experience. Yet assent and thrill so enters into all dramatic utterance, that the threat of the poetic reality to take over all other realms of human reality is fearful. In *The Structure of Rime I*, it came to me in writing that *"a snake-like beauty in the living changes of syntax"* spoke, and cried;

> *Jacob wrestled with Sleep—you who fall into Nothingness and dread Sleep.*
> *He wrestled with Sleep like a man reading a strong sentence.*

It has seemed to me that I wrestle with the syntax of the world of my experience to bring forward into the Day the twisted syntax of my human language that will be changed in that contest even with what I dread there. And recently I have come to think of Poetry more and more as a wrestling with Form to liberate Form. The figure of Jacob returns again and again to my thought.

"J'ai dit *fictions*," Festugière writes in *La Révélation d'Hermès Trismégiste*: "car, pour nous, modernes, il est évident que les récits hellénistiques de révélation ne comportent aucun fond de vérité." William James in his *Principles of Psychology* (chapter xxi, p. 292) among the seven realms of reality that the philosopher must take into account, lists as the fifth a realm of fiction: "the various supernatural worlds, the Christian heaven and hell, the world of the Hindoo mythology, the world of Swedenborg's *visa et audita*, etc." And concludes: "The various worlds of deliberate fable may be ranked with these worlds of faith—the world of the *Iliad*, that of *King Lear*, of the *Pickwick Papers*." In a footnote on the reality of this realm of fictions, taking the novel *Ivanhoe* as example, James's account becomes more immediate:

> Whilst absorbed in the novel, we turn our backs on all other worlds, and, for the time, the Ivanhoe-world remains our absolute reality. When we wake from that spell, however, we find a still more real world, which reduces *Ivanhoe*, and all things connected with him, to the fictive status, and relegates them to one of the sub-universes grouped under No. 5.

This experience of waking up from a spell, from one reality into a *real* or *true* reality, waking up from a dream into the consciousness of daily life, liberated from the overwhelming creature-feeling one has in dream, as if one were being dreamt, in-bound to the fateful or plot-full (meaningful, the Freudian might add) design of the dream, to the household and work-a-day world of comfortable or suitable procedures, is experienced in reverse by the convert to psychoanalysis, who begins to find in dreams, or, rather, in his interpretation of dreams, the real tenor of daily life. Now, not only are dreams the stuff life is made of, but life is the stuff dreams are made of. And in the psychopathology of daily life, the still more real world of the actual begins to be a text of meanings, actions that reveal ritual intention, symbolic functions, words and appearances that are not what they seem. The work-a-day world, if we but hear, speaks in tongues, and the waking consciousness casts a spell of its own in awakeness, at once revealing the true nature of things and concealing it.

So too, not only Freudian converts but Christian converts awake from sleep, come alive from death, see the light of day after the dark of night, and find "a still more real world." Waking up and coming to our senses, back to the world as it is figured in our sensory systems or our inner organic consciousness, seems to be solid information. Here, surely, reality is embodied, spirit is incarnate. But whatever realm of reality we seek out, we find it is woven of fictions. Endlessly, philosophy unwinds the threads to tell the more real from the merely real, the final nature of every impression—what is substantial? what is essential? what is idea? And what seems most authoritative to "modern" man, the picture of our human physiology and of the universe as it is hypothesized in scientific thought, calls into question our senses, undoes as an illusion what we still feel we "wake" to in our daily lives.

When I try to remember, before learning to read for myself, first hearings of poetry, what comes immediately to illustrate—it must be set in the pattern of things it comes so readily—is my sitting with my sister, my mother between us, looking at the pictures in a book as my mother reads aloud. The picture I am looking at is of three young men sleeping on a mat. One of them, the poet Bashō, has awakened. Their naked feet are uncovered where they have pulled the blankets up around their necks in the cold. There is a poem that goes

[17]

with that picture on the page. But this is not the poem that comes to mind even as I see the picture. For as I remember that moment, there is another scene superimposed, a double exposure, in which the very plash of a frog jumping into an old pond appears as if from actual life itself, but this vivid impression belongs to one of the most famous of all Japanese *hokkus*:

> The old pond,—aye!
> A frog leapt into it,—
> List, the water sound!

I am embarrassed now by the diction as I seek out the poem in *Little Pictures of Japan,* edited by Olive Beaupré Miller in 1925. The illustrations for that volume were by Katharine Sturges, whose work today is still fresh, having the high style of the 1920s and rich and subtle color, drawn from the Japanese palette. And I find too that the poem—even in this translation (that now seems to my taste unfortunately mannered) the vehicle of a living experience—and the picture of the three Japanese poets that first came to my mind belong together in that early moment. For the picture is on the following page. As my mother turned the page and my eyes were caught by the drawing of Bashō and his friends huddled in bed, the image of the frog-pond-sound poem was still vivid, or, perhaps, growing more vivid in my imagination.

Why do I digress here to rediscover the time and place in my thought of that poem? What I had written in the first draft of this essay, from which I am working and reworking as I type here, was:

> When I try to remember back of first school, there is the plash of the frog jumping into Bashō's pond from Olive Beaupré Miller's *Little Pictures of Japan* . . .

The picture of the sleeping young men does not come into

[18]

that account at all. It did come to my mind as I wrote, but I dismissed it, for I could not see that it belonged. I interfered with the shape of things. I could not see the good of it, until, after writing, I went to the book to find the poem that had come and found then that the seemingly inconsequent picture did indeed belong to the order of that first impression. Once the sequence had been restored, the configuration leads on.

What followed the passage above in the notebook is:

sitting with my mother reading, my sister and I gazing at the pictures . . .

How puzzling it was to be seeing then the picture of three poets, even as I meant to evoke the first poem and from the world of images there was the frog jumping, I was looking into the world of pictures and seeing the drawing again, and beyond, the scene where we were that afternoon, the three of us as if we were on a stage, the room from so long ago furnished as if in stage-directions:

. . . beyond the picture window the rectangular [*I had wanted to say* oblong, *but the word called up some childhood doubt of whether one could say that word for . . . for . . . and then the word* rectangular *came. The very sound of* oblong *seemed childishly too deliteful to be right.*]
. . . beyond the picture window the rectangular pond with its flowing fountain.

Working here now I returned to consider the very book, to refresh my experience, and to honor the creative intent of Olive Beaupré Miller, who edited the series called *The Book House for Children,* as one of the great educators of the nineteen-twenties, and the beauty of Katharine Sturges's work, that has style, high style, and sensuality, and the full magic of color, because the very book—the feel of its binding, the smell of its pages—has taken its place as a thing of my life story. So much so, that it seemed to me to have been there long before

I was six. Often, in researching what is for us eternal, we are puzzled indeed to find that it has an historical limit. There was just this time and just this place each actual moment and scene is. Very early indeed I was told and then read, before I could read, the story of Cupid and Psyche. I am always astonished to find that it is not in Hawthorne's *Wonder Book* which out of my nursery days seems to me to be an ancient, a primordial collection. Interrupting again to search out where among my childhood books I would have found it, it is not in *My Book House*, but . . . there! I find what could have been the book, for it was among my childhood books: *Myths from Many Lands*, the second volume in *The Children's Hour* set. But nothing about the book as I hold it reawakens a time or times of having read this story there. The locus in reading of *Cupid and Psyche* comes later in my life story, for it belongs to my mature and studious reading of that myth in the very text (but I, having no Latin, must speak of the translation of the very text), in the context of its origin in *The Golden Ass* or *The Transformations of Lucius* by Lucius Apuleius.

Cupid and Psyche not only has its origins in what patently is a fiction or romance, "clothing a reality", we may suspect or allow, and containing perhaps things known in mystery cult but proposed as an entertainment, and in a work of fiction whose origin is not lost itself in the well of memory, as the origin of the *Iliad* or the *Theogony* of Hesiod or *Genesis* is lost, far back of the writing down of these works, in an oral tradition that precedes Greek or Hebrew records, but belongs, as the Gospels of the New Testament, orthodox and apocryphal, do, to the embarrassment of historical time. In the terms given by Apuleius' novel itself, the myth appears as an old wives' tale. "*I, however, will immediately recall you from grief, by pleasant narrations, and old women's fables,*" the old midwife of the story says in Thomas Taylor's translation. "*However, I will proceed to divert you, by some pretty stories, and old women's tales,*" the anonymous translator for the Bohn Library version has it. *"Now let me tell you a fairy tale or two to make you feel a little better,"* the poet Robert Graves, who believes the whole novel is informed by religious experience and purpose, translates.

My purpose in going back of the simple presentation of the original version I am working from in my notebooks, back to bring into play the actual volume, *the very book,* and the context of a childhood library, then, following the lead as it came, to trace to its place the story of Cupid and Psyche—my purpose here has been to give some idea of how little a matter of "free" association and how much a matter of an enduring design in which the actual living consciousness arises, how much a matter of actual times and actual objects the living reality of the myth is for the poet. Just these times, just these objects, just these persons come to mind—at once things-in-themselves and things in ourselves. One has not to reach for them often, and, even reaching for them, it is these that come. The surety of the myth for the poet has such force that it operates as a primary reality in itself, having volition. The mythic content comes to us, commanding the design of the poem; it calls the poet into action, and with whatever lore and craft he has prepared himself for that call, he must answer to give body in the poem to the formative will.

For the Bororo people who live immersed in myth, Claude Lévi-Strauss tells us, the myths themselves are *persons.* In a true telling of the story there is a reincarnation of the story, the vehicle of the myth in a new life. The hearer, lost in the very presence of the myth—recall here how the awkward translation of Bashō's poem was yet the body of its presence for the child listening: pond, frog and splash were enduringly encoded—even as he enjoys the art of the storyteller or maker, becomes converted to the reality of the story; in the full enchantment of art, fiction has the depth and lastingness as a real experience that actuality has only in events of like creative participation. Yet in the failure of that creative immediacy, we will come to feel that the story is not true to itself. Instead of the very myth, we feel we are presented with a portrait; its truth, a likeness. In childhood, we did not want a word changed or the order of words in their sentences changed, any more than we wanted an unfamiliar expression in those closest to us or a change in the order of things about us. This is the mystery of impersonations: we cease to see the variety of what we love in order to recognize. "Though men associate with it most closely," Heraclitus says of the Law (*Logos*), "yet they are separated from it, and those things which they encounter daily seem to them strange." Looking upon the actual lineaments of my companion's face and head, I find I have trespassed upon alien areas of what I most love, and grow afraid. We domesticate, civilize, idealize, characterize, humanize ourselves and all that is "ours"; taking identity in what we can command. This house commands a view of the valley. Great ceremonies, rituals, paradigms, pentacles, perspectives, strive to bring into the command of a little room titanic or demonic powers, to define time and space, to give primordial form— the process of reality to which cosmos and life belong—a conventional form. In periods of greatest panic, such as the eighteenth century following the nightmare religious enthusiasms and wars of the seventeenth, the form tolerable to convention can shrink to a tennis court. But there remains the deepest drive of the artist, a yearning to participate in the primordial reality that challenges the boundaries of convention and the purposes of pedagogy again and again. In the orders of the poem the poet is commanded by necessities of a form that will not be turned to exemplify moral or aesthetic preconceptions. (Writing, one follows through a series of events having their own imperative.) So myths—the story of Enkidu and Gilgamesh, the story of Adam and Eve and the Garden of Eden, the story of Ouranos, Kronos, and Zeus—resist our interpretations and understandings and confound our philosophies.

How often those most concerned with us, who most love us or most hate us, can come to feel that we are not true to our real selves. In the tragedy of religious convictions, where men have tortured and killed to force others or themselves to come to the true faith, the depth and bitterness of this feeling of the truth of life or story or man to which life or story or man may play false is written in terrible acts. Today we play out in East Asia all the grievous patterns once enacted in Catholic crusades against gnostics and Jews or Protestant persecutions of Catholics and witches. The very inspiration that carries the artist through in a state that combines fear for form and faith in form to realize the imperatives of his poem, moves makers of history who write their works in the lives of men. Hitler moves as the wrath of God to show a terrible truth about Germany, about Europe, about our Western Christian civilization itself; as Johnson today betrays the character of Babbitt swollen with his opportunity in history. Where history becomes myth, men are moved not toward the ends they desire but toward their fates, the ends they deserve.

Yet our lives and works are not simply what they are but are passively or actively, unconsciously or consciously, creative of what they are. The universe strives to be what it truly is to be. The poem that moves me when I write is an active presence in which I work. I am not concerned with whether it is a good or a bad likeness to some convention men hold; for the Word is for me living Flesh, and the body of my own thought and feeling, my own presence, becomes the vehicle for the process of genetic information.

Plato in *The Symposium* saw man's works as his spiritual progeny. There are artists who would work and rework the creative code of our human chromosomes in a test-tube to produce model homunculi; poets whose babes are contrived to perfect their own nature, civilized and formed, as Dryden would edit Shakespeare, to conform to the tastes and conventions of reasonable men. Plato argued that the poets lied in their myths because they showed gods not to be good. And many Christians have twisted the poetry of the Bible in vices of interpretation to see the divine as conforming to our highest ethical precepts, and, where their humanitarian ideals were strong, come to apostasy when faced with the immoveable reality of Jehovah who declares Himself a God of Jealousy, Vengence and Wrath. Reason falters, but our mythic, our deepest poetic sense, recognizes and greets as truth the proclamation that the Son brings that just this Wrathful Father is the First Person of Love. As Chaos, the Yawning Abyss, is First Person of Form. And the Poet too, like the Son, in this myth of Love or Form, must go deep into the reality of His own Nature, into the Fathering Chaos or Wrath, to suffer His own Nature. In this mystery of the art, the Son's cry to the Father might be too the cry of the artist to the form he obeys.

It has never seemed to me that the true form of a poem was a convention or an ideal of form, but, as in life, a form having its information in the language of our human experience, as our bodies have their information in the life-code of the species, and our spirit in the creative will. The individual poem stirs in our minds, an event in our language, as the individual embryonic cell stirs in the parent body. The beginning of the poem stirs in every area of my consciousness, for the DNA code it will use toward its incarnation is a code of resources my life pattern itself carries; not only thought and feeling but all the nervous and visceral and muscular intelligences of the body are moved. Awakening—listening, seeing, sensing—to work with the moving weights and durations of syllables, the equilibrations of patterns, the liberations of new possibilities of movement; to cooperate in the aroused process. Attending.

From the first inspiration, breathing *with* the new breath. Man's myths move in his poetry as they move in his history, as in the morphology of his body all his ancient evolution is rehearsed and individualized; all of vertebrate imagination moves to create itself anew in his spine. Families of men like families of gods are the creative grounds of key persons. And all mankind share the oldest gods as they share the oldest identities of the germinal cell. This share is so real that even the most racial tribalism—the ethnocentric laws of Ezra—cannot render the Jews other than or more than men; and Jahweh for the Christians is the Father, one of Three Persons in the Nature of God. For those of us who search out the widest imagination of our manhood—our piety must seem as appalling to the Christians as the Christian's piety is to the Jews— God strives in all Creation to come to Himself. The Gods men know are realizations of God. But what I speak of here in the terms of a theology is a poetics. Back of each poet's concept of the poem is his concept of the meaning of form itself; and his concept of form in turn where it is serious at all arises from his concept of the nature of the universe, its lifetime or form, or even, for some, its lifelessness or formlessness. A mystic cosmogony gives rise to the little world the poet as creator makes.

When in the inception of *A Poem Beginning with a Line by Pindar*, reading late at night the third line of the first Pythian Ode in the translation by Wade-Gery and Bowra, my mind lost the hold of Pindar's sense and was faced with certain puns, so that the words *light, foot, hears, you, brightness, begins* moved in a world beyond my reading, these were no longer words alone but also powers in a theogony, having resonances in Hesiodic and Orphic cosmogonies where the foot that moves in the dance of the poem appears as the pulse of measures in first things. Immediately, sight of Goya's great canvas, once seen in the Marquis de Cambo's collection in Barcelona, came to me, like a wave, carrying the vision—out of the evocation of the fragment from Pindar and out of Goya's pictorial evocation to add their masterly powers to my own—the living vision, Cupid and Psyche, were there; then, the power of a third master, not a master of poetry or of picture but of story-telling, the power of Lucius Apuleius was there too. In the grand theurgy of picture and story, the living genius of these three stood as my masters, and I stood in the very presence of the story of Cupid and Psyche—but, in the power of those first Words—Light, Foot, Hears, You, Brightness, Begins—He was the primal Eros, and she, the First Soul. Waking into the reality of the poem, so that the room where I wrote, the fact that I was writing, and the catalytic process of the works of art, passed into the process of the poem itself, dimly underlying the work, as in actual life we may be aware that dream processes are at work, the poem as I wrote forming such a powerful nexus or vehicle of this transcendent reality of Eros and Psyche and of the revelations flowing out of the myth they belonged to, I was hard pressed to keep up with the formations as they came. I cannot make it happen or want it to happen; it wells up in me as if I were a point of break-thru for an "I" that may be any person in the cast of a play, that may like the angel speaking to Caedmon command "Sing me some thing." When that "I" is lost, when the voice of the poem is lost, the matter of the poem, the intense information of the content, no longer comes to me, then I know I have to wait until that voice returns. The return is felt as a readiness, a body tone. One of the disciplines I have struggled to achieve and struggle still to achieve is a quickness to recognize shifts in the nature of the work, to stop, even in mid-air, when I have lost the feel, for the reality of the poem—the creative nexus or the true poem that moves the poem—is the source, not the product, of my working there. In the imperative of Poetry three forces move to incarnate themselves in the poem: the words, come alive in their resonances of sound, pulse and meaning—this is the reservoir of our humanity; the life experience and imagination of the poet—this is the reservoir of his craft and recognitions, the range of his creation of person; and the actual body of the poet—the reservoir of his life-style. But name two First Movers of the poem. Name Seven. Name the Seventy-Two. In every configuration the Myth of the Poem will write itself anew.

Many a young poet comes to his vocation today the product of a demythologized education. The separation of Church and State has been interpreted to mean that the lore of God is the matter of the private individual, and the myths of the Old and New Testament are no longer part of our common learning. Rationalizing scientists have conducted a war against fairytales and phantasies. Myth can be allowed as an element of personal expression in creative art, but myth as an inherited lore of the soul-way of Man has been put aside. The modifiers "primal" and "deep" come as we try to convey that the mythopoeic may be of anthropological or psychological value; yet for the poet the common property of man's myths is a resource of working material, a grammar of rimes. A young poet who had studied *A Poem Beginning with a Line by Pindar* discovered that the myth of *Cupid and Psyche* was not a "deep" myth, nor an ancient one, but no more than a tale told in a novel by Apuleius. This "fairytale", as Apuleius himself labels it, is for me not only the fable embodying the doctrine of the soul, as Thomas Taylor tells us in his note, "*evidently* alluded to by Synesius, in his book on Dreams, and *obscurely* by Plato and Plotinus", the very primordial pattern from which the life of the soul—philosophies and stories and poetries—flows, but it is also, what it first was, a bed-time story. The depths emerge in a kind of dream informed by the familiar tale. It is important here that the myth be first so familiar, so much no-more-than an old story, that the poet is at home with what is most perilous.

Concentrating on the constructions of the poem, following the workings out of sound and content, in order to cooperate fully with what is given, the poet is protected from what might otherwise disturb his personality. His intellect intent upon the ratios and movements of the poem, he is almost unaware of depths that may be stirred in his own psyche. What he feels is the depth and excitement of the poem. The poem takes over. When I—

Just before I started here quickly to recall the working of the poem at the time of writing, thinking of the primordial as the flowing fountain I had seen before or recalled in the garden outside the room where we two children sat with our mother reading, when I came that close, I came close upon weeping. And I remember how I wondered at George Herbert's theme of weeping in so many poems of *The Temple*. I thought then—this was in 1945 when I read Herbert in the sense of my own unrequited love and I too wept—it was in grief for the agony of Man's sin which Christ had taken upon Himself on the Cross. But I was raised to feel things in the terms of *karma* according to my parents' theosophy or in terms of *shame* from their middle-class worship of social status; I was not prepared to think in terms of sin. Now, I would understand sin as Man's refusal of Love Itself, his refusal to love in his desire to have love—my own human refusal of the love that strives to speak in the poem. Not only the loss of love, which confronts us, where we admit the suffering, with the reality of love, but the recognition of love moves us to tears. Our daily affections are a gentle practiced removal from a reality that threatens to overcome us. Our sexual pleasure is a protective appetite that distracts us or blinds the psyche to the primal Eros, as all the preoccupations of our poetic craft preserve a skin of consciousness in which we are not overtaken in fear of the Form that works there.

In my manly years, I weep for pain and in the pain of others, and for grief; and I weep for the power of works of art that break the reserves of my aesthetic and stand in the immediacy of first experience, and I weep for the courage of noble men. Now it comes to me that George Herbert, whose poems are addressed so directly to his Christ, whose poems are prayers and do not have the protective remove that the poem as a work of art has or the poem as projected by the poet to his imaginary reader or hearer has, it comes to me that George Herbert wept as just now, as I touched in writing some chord in the conjunction of that actual fountain in the garden long ago and the myth thought of as belonging to the order of another fountain, a fountain of living forms, and these arising in melody from the pond-frog-plash first poem, releasing an unbearable nearness—

> Garcia Lorca stole
> poetry from this drinking-fountain

I wrote in one of the poems of *Caesar's Gate*—I almost came to weeping as I wrote and had to retreat from the idea as best I could. *Idea*, for me, is not something I have but something that comes to me or appears to me; as in Plato, a thing *seen*. The fountain, and Eros and Psyche, the two persons of Apuleius's fairytale—this is what the young man misunderstood—are not made-up things but numinous. The numen is not only awe-full; it moves us to tears.

Modern man, the very modern man who, so Bultmann argues, will accept the kerygma of Christianity, if only the myth-trouble may be removed, has labeled whole areas of human thought and feeling sentimental and over-charged with improper emotion or emoting, in order to escape from the threat of discomposing images or affections. *Is that true or do you only imagine it?* he demands. *You do not truly feel that.* He has erected an education of sensibility, class spirit or team spirit, argument and rationalization, designed to establish himself in a self-protective world of facts and problems stripped of their sympathies, in the real business of making money, serving and protecting the system of private property and capital or public property and capital, and exploiting the profitable waste, substituting his own person for soul, until the whole bag of swollen vulture's wind and meat threatens to consume our lives. For many, only tears of exasperation are left. Despair has no tears.

"Can Christian preaching expect modern man *to accept* . . . ?" . . . "It is impossible to use electric light and the wireless and to avail ourselves of modern medical and surgical discoveries, and at the same time . . ." —so the voice of Bultmann's manifesto goes bravely on: Myth "as such . . . is simply the cosmology of a pre-scientific age." The voice he impersonates here is a voice that has again and again, sneering or pitying or condescending, reproved the poet for his pathetic fallacies, his phantasmagoria, his personifications, ecstatic realizations, pretensions. When Bultmann tells us that "Myth speaks of the power or the powers which man *supposes* he experiences," he reproves the imagination itself. He would be admonishing Ezra Pound for pretending such things are real in Canto 91:

> that the body of light come forth
>   from the body of fire
> And that your eyes come to the surface
>   from the deep wherein they were sunken,
> Reina—for 300 years,
>   and now sunken
> That your eyes come forth from their caves
>   & light then
>   as the holly-leaf
>   qui laborat, orat.

The poet cannot *suppose* he sees, though, it is true, seeing may arise from the evocation of "suppose I see. . ." However he pretends or supposes he sees, he either does or does not see in that pretension. We recognize an image in the process of the poem not because of some device of speech, not as a descriptive arrangement of words or a striking word, but because we see as we write. In the memory of the first poem and the picture, the poem, moving the imagination, was remembered as an actual experience of a frog leaping and the plash of the pond; the picture actually seen by my eyes was remembered as a picture seen. May there not be a hint that what we experience in our actual life is also what has entered the imagination and there been imagined as experience? In memory, it is my imagination of the three of us seen as if from slightly above, seeing even myself, sitting there, that illustrates my experience.

"Sentimentality" is often the accusation brought by the critic when he would refuse some experience or ideal arising in the poem that does not satisfy or support his personal world of values but would threaten, if it were allowed, to undo that world. The word *sentimental* means "supposed" experience, I suppose. "You do not really feel that" or "you are letting your feelings get away with you" is the reproof often where we would not like to allow the feeling detected to advance, lest we too feel what the advancing feeling brings with it. Much of modern criticism of poetry is not to raise a crisis in our consideration of the content or to deepen our apprehension of the content, but to dismiss the content. When such critics would bring the flight of imagination down to earth, they mean not the earth men have revered and worked with love and awe, the imagined earth, but the real estate modern man has made of Earth for his own uses.

This modern man so speaks in me that, as, in writing of the fictional or romantic or mythic fountain, I became disturbed by the sight of that fountain forming, my first thought of retreat from the image came with this modern critical thought that I had begun to sentimentalize so that I got weepy with my own emoting. I sprang up from the thought then to turn to the actual book not only to refresh my sense of the evocative scene, but to bring it down to earth, to the sight, the feel, the smell of an objective fact to give physical bounds to that evocation. I shied away from the idea of the fountain of living souls. Only my life experience in the imagination, my times when I have held steady to see, if only for the fragment of a second, and the times when commands have come that I did not dare meet ordering me to hold steady in seeing, and the acknowledgement of the truth of what I have seen, "supposed" I saw, in reading Proclus, compelled me to admit, beyond my sense of contemporary proprieties, that it was not "sentimental" to come upon weeping as one came upon seeing.

The modern mind has not only chickened out on God, on angels, on Creation, but it has chickened out on the common things of our actual world, taking the properties of things as their uses and retracting all sense of fellow creatureliness. Not only the presences of gods and of ideas are denied, becoming for the modern man "supposed" experiences, but the presences of stones, trees, animals and even men as spiritual beings is exorcised in our contemporary common sense. Wherever this contempt moves, it strikes to constrict the realm of empathy. And we see a middle-class meanness of mind that not only rejects from consideration high-flying lordly pretensions— thought that is moved by the grandeur of the universe, time beyond the time of man and space beyond the solar system, the rose of light that Dante in the heights of his vision saw and the abyss before light that Hesiod tells us just as it was remains first in Creation—but likewise dismisses all consideration of spiritual being in humble persons. Man may see by symbols, reading meanings into things and events; much of what he

[32]

calls experience arises from purely verbal activity. There can be no true significance, no sign that mineral or plant can give in which we have a proper communion, no language whereby things may speak to us. Where the whole field of human experience is man's own, psychology and semantics take over. Signs are no longer presences but poetic sentimentalities, mere fancies, or, wherever men still would speak with the world about them and take the universe into his councils, symptoms of psychopathology.

"The sentimentality destroys some of the poems," a recent mentor of poetic proprieties writes of Denise Levertov's work:

> It is not sentimentality about the poor, her troubles, dying rabbits or sunsets, but rather sentimentality about words like "seraphic" and "demonic." Subway entrances become "steps to the underworld." In *From the Roof* she says: "who can say | the crippled broom-vendor yesterday, who passed | just as we needed a new broom, was not | one of the Hidden Ones?"

"Who indeed?" then the contemptuous critic sneers. Does he suppose he is dismissing out of hand the silly personal fancy of the poetess? He seems ignorant of the world of Jewish mysticism, the generations of a living community to which Denise Levertov's imagination here belongs, and into which, through her father, rabbi and then Christian priest, translator of the Zohar, she was born. But he is not ignorant, for referring to another poem, "Illustrious Ancestors", he grows scornful here of her pretension as he sees it to some spiritual claim. Actually, in the poem, remembering her paternal ancestor the Rav of Northern White Russia and her maternal ancestor Angel Jones of Mold, she lays no claim but *"Well, I would like to make, | thinking some line still taut between me and them, | poems direct as what the birds said,*

hard as a floor, sound as a bench
mysterious as the silence when the tailor
would pause with his needle in the air.

But for the modern demythologizing mind, our sense of a life shared with the beings of a household, our sense of belonging to generations of spirit, our ancestral pieties, must be put aside. And then, back of the critic's outrage at this poem, was the fact that he was confronted again by such as the broom vendor: for meditations of Angel Jones, Denise Levertov tells us, *"were sewn into coats and britches."*

"In the rather prosaic life of these poems," the critic protests: *"the truth is that a broom vendor is a broom vendor."* He does not seem aware that it is in his own eyes that the life of these poems becomes "rather prosaic" nor that he shows forth in his contempt for the thought at all that a mere broom vendor might be *"one of the Hidden Ones"* a hubris that is fearful.

In the belief in the Hidden Zaddik, the divine wisdom that the least of men may be illumined by, the Chassidic masters speak not only to the Jewish community but to our common humanity. In the fairy tales of every people there are stories of those who will not recognize in the wretched and contemptible even, the presence of a divine life. A little Clod of Clay, *"trodden with the cattle's feet"*, sings in Blake's poem:

Love seeketh not Itself to please,
Nor for itself hath any care,
But for another gives its ease,
And builds a Heaven in Hell's despair.

"That is only a fairytale! The truth is. . ." Our modern-minded critic here is that very proud, ugly and ungracious stepsister, eager to see through the pretentiousness of things, who, directed to the source of treasure, finds Mother Hulda to be only a tiresome old housewife and the work that Mother Hulda asks of her to be no more than dreary tasks. Our whole

American Way of Life is designed to save the householder from his household myths, from the lifestory of working in which he has his communion with the house; as in the factory, the worker, no longer a maker, is removed from his work. Works become commodities, and the ends of labor, not in the grains of the field or the goods produced, but in the wages, benefits and social approval earned. Tables and chairs, *"the house, the fruit, the grape,"* that the poet Rilke saw, *"into which the hope and meditation of our forefathers had entered,"* become props. "Now there come crowding over from America empty, indifferent things, pseudo-things, dummy-life," Rilke writes: "The animated, experienced things that share our lives are coming to an end and cannot be replaced."

It is the very idea that there is a miraculous grace ever about us, a mystery of person, that our modern critic refuses to allow. Personality takes the place of the individual living soul. The broom vendor or the Vietnamese Communist has not earned or has forfeited his reality as a person. *"A holy man becomes a holy man only by incredible physical sacrifice,"* Denise Levertov's critic admonishes. This is the very voice of the Protestant ethic as Weber defined it in his *Capitalism and the Protestant Ethic.* The presumption can only increase:

> Denise Levertov wants to have a prosaic housewiferly life, and find her kitchen step-ladder in Jacob's Ladder. It won't work. Her reading of the lives of saints is sentimental.

Everywhere there is the ready suspicion and accusation that the poet has not really *earned* or *deserved* to have wonder manifest in the poem, as if wonder came from some power of the writer's and was not a grace recognized by the writer in the reality of things. The world then is filled with "prosaic" things, broom vendors, housewiferly life, and kitchen step-ladders, that do not deserve our poetic attentions, or that need to be seen as deep images of the psyche before they become poetic. As things in themselves, they won't work.

For career poets, both the Jacob's Ladder, the stairway of rosy stone *"that takes | a glowing tone of softness,"* that Denise Levertov sees in her poem, where angels' feet *"only glance in their tread, and need not | touch the stone,"* but where a man *"climbing | must scrape his knees, and bring | the grip of his hands into play,"* and the household kitchen ladder, are high-minded or trivial sentimentalities in light of the very real ladder of status. Where, looking upward, the ambitious professional sees spirits elevated above their just deserts and, looking downward, sees spirits who had better not put on airs.

The folktale was itself the very lowly, simple, or, like Bearskin or the Toad-Prince, beastly and despised shape in whom the true heart would have its groom; and princes and princesses in fairytales come to their kingdoms only after lives in anonymous wandering and servitude, tending swine, sitting among the cinders. Back of fairytale is the despised life of the peasant.

Myth comes bringing to our minds the realm of great powers, ceremonies of primal Kings. Its persons are beyond our human condition, movers of the universe and initiators of first mysteries. The makers of myth have the grandeur of ancient time surrounding them, they are sages or mages more famous than kings. Homer, Hesiod, the priests at Saïs and in Sumer, or the mythic Orpheus and Hermes who invented the lyre, god of thieves, liars and poets, or the shamans climbing the ladder of visions to make that trip to the other world and bring back the soul's story, these still belong to the orders of our lordly pretentions. Great myth has its home in great places, inspired from the Abyss or from Heaven, told from the tripod or altar, in temple or sacred grove. It may be seen as the remnant of once glorious but now perverted and heathen religion.

But folk and fairytale have their home in the gossip of old wives and little children, stories about the cooking-hearth and the nursery bedside. Whatever remnant there was in folktale of religion it must have fallen far even from heathen perversion to come so into the contemptible ignorance of the people. Myth was populated by monsters, which men with higher minds might interpret in theosophies or philosophies, psychologies or etymologies to convey transcendent or deeper meanings. It might be primitive science or primitive history in which the record of great events and speculations was written. But the lowly folktale was populated irremediably by kitchen sluts and begging women and broom vendors and soldiers home from the wars and the like and their wish-phantasies and fear-delusions.

Myth might spring from the Imagination that Coleridge calls primary: "the living Power and prime Agent of all human Perception", and as such belongs to the order of high Poetry. But folk and fairytale then belong to what Coleridge is concerned to demote as Fancy, to the order of Otway's *"Lutes, lobsters, seas of milk, and ships of amber"*. Its supernatural beings are insignificant, sub-natural, really: fairies, elves, and animal spirits belong to lower orders in nature than mankind.

So, it seems, the modern man whose concern Bultmann would woo dismisses the mythology of a cosmic Christ, but another Christ, the Jesus of folktale and legend, the very fairytale hero in the New Testament who is a lowly carpenter, an unrecognized king, whose kingdom, like fairyland, is not of this world, and whose disciples are despised men and women, does not seem to come into the question at all. He is beneath our intellectual consideration. For this Christ speaks not to our intellects but to our human sentiments. He moves the heart.

In the nineteenth century, scholars of the myth and the folktale battled to claim territory for the humble story-teller in the great poetry of the Iliad and the Mahabharata or to lay claim for the sublime shaman-poet or priest of the solar cult in nursery rime and fairytale, as Müller saw ritual mysteries of freeing the dawn's light in the tale of Jason and Medea and the Golden Fleece, and Lang saw a swineherd's phantasies in the *Odyssey*. But in Germany, poets—Tieck, Goethe, Hoffmann, Novalis—had written myths and fairytales that came not from the ground of lost religion nor from the ground of the folk but from the ground of a fictional imagination that we recognize as Romanticism. The very word "Romantic" is, in literary and social criticism today, pejorative. But it is in the Romantic vein—to which I see my own work as clearly belonging—that the two worlds, the lordly and the humble, that seemed to scholars irreconcilably at odds, mythological vision and folklorish phantasy, are wedded in a phantasmagoria —as Goethe called his Helen episode—the spiritual romance. This wedding of higher orders and lower orders has a prototype in the Greek theater, where high tragedy and the satyr play belonged together, and today, over a hundred years after the beginnings of the Romantic synthesis, our poetic task remains to compose the true epithalamium where chastity and lewdness, love and lust, the philosopher king and the monstrous clown dance together in all their human reality.

In England, the divine Blake broke through the confines of seventeenth- and eighteenth-century rationalist poetics with his *Marriage of Heaven and Hell*, blasting that model of self-righteous and reasonable men, the Deist, and howling against the first factories and machineries of his own day's versions of what Bultmann considers to be the modern scientific man for whom: "it is impossible to use electric light and the wireless and to avail ourselves of modern medical and surgical discoveries, and at the same time to believe in the New Testament world of spirits and miracles. . . . What matters is the world view which men imbibe from their environment, and it is science which determines that view of the world through the school, the press, the wireless, the cinema, and all other fruits of technical progress." For the illuminati of this kind of rationalism, all spiritual men seem to have regressed into the irrational darkness of primitive mind.

Myth, for Dante, for Shakespeare, for Milton, was the poet-lore handed down in the tradition from poet to poet. It was the very matter of Poetry, the nature of the divine world as poets had testified to it; the poetic piety of each poet, his acknowledgment of what he had found true Poetry, worked to conserve that matter. And, for each, there was in the form of their work—the literary vision, the play of actors upon the stage, and the didactic epic—a kind of magic, for back of these forms we surmise distant origins in the rituals toward ecstasy of earliest Man. Once the operations of their art began they were transported from their sense of myth as a literary element into the immediacy of the poem where reality was mythological. In the *Divine Comedy*, moving back of actual time and space (and, I would recall here that Dante makes a fiction, an artful dodge in actual time for his Vision, for he pre-dates his poem so that he continually has foreknowledge after the event, as in his stanzas he fore-rhymes) in the tradition of the Descent Into Hell and Ascent To Heaven poem, a form that has its remote origins in shamanistic practice, and its myth in the story of Orpheus, Dante "finds himself" in a dark wood. The leopard, the lion, and the she-wolf are charged with allegorical meaning; but with Dante always the meaning is more than one; the fictive proposition is also visionary reality. He figures ratios of actual time and place that are poetic measures. The actual world is filled with messages, and actual persons give signs.

Shakespeare too has a magic, the magic of the stage. And such will be his persuasion that from that extention of reality into myth he tells us that the actual world itself is but a stage and we are therein in a play called life. So too, the vast theatrical space projected in the opening passages of Milton's *Paradise Lost* is mythic architecture, passing from artifice into a felt dimension, given by the depth of Satan's fall, where again the fictional form operates to move the poet and the reader into an "other" space in the reality of which actual space fades.

With Blake, the poet's sense of his primordial inspiration, his coexistence in the original time of spiritual beings and in the very presence of powers, appears in his actual life itself. He does not write poems as ways into the mythological; he writes poems *from* the realm of that reality. But this sense of spiritual immediacies, the here-and-now of First Things and Last Things, is not Blake's alone. Let me take the Romantic proposition from the pages of Coleridge's *Biographia Literaria:*

> To find no contradiction in the union of old and new; to contemplate the *Ancient* of days and all his works with feelings as fresh, as if all had then sprung forth at the first creative fiat; characterizes the mind that feels the riddle of the world, and may help to unravel it. To carry on the feelings of childhood into the powers of manhood; to combine the child's sense of wonder and novelty with the appearances, which every day for perhaps forty years had rendered familiar:
>
> > With sun and moon and stars throughout the year,
> > And man and woman;
>
> this is the character and privilege of genius, and one of the marks which distinguish genius from talents.

Then he speaks of the poet as rescuing

> the most admitted truths from the impotence caused by the very circumstance of their universal admission. Truths of all others the most awful and mysterious, yet being at the same time of universal interest, are too often considered as *so* true, that they lose all the life and efficiency of truth, and lie bed-ridden in the dormitory of

the soul, side by side with the most despised and exploded errors.

Coleridge and Wordsworth, as well as Blake, significantly revive the admiration of the soul in its lowly and outcast experience—"the most despised and exploded errors" of humanity, such could seem to righteous middle-class minds. The poor laborer, the ignorant cottager, the demented mariner, the child—these appear in the Romantic Imagination as the Hidden Zaddik appeared in the romantic imagination of the Chassidic masters.

"Awake!" "Awake!" Blake cries.

Sometime in 1953, the poetess Helen Adam brought Blake's introductory song from *Songs of Experience* as an example of great poetry to a workshop and read it in a sublime and visionary manner, as if what was important was not the accomplishment of the poem but the wonder of the world of the poem itself, breaking the husk of my modernist pride and shame, my conviction that what mattered was the literary or artistic achievement. It may be that nothing will ever remove that husk, but its triumph is broken. Whatever I think of devices of the art, of metaphor and simile, of development of themes and composition, when I speak of resonances I mean that the music of the poem—a music of sounds and of meanings—awakens the mythological reality in the actual; and when I speak of form I mean not something the poet gives to things but something he receives from things. We are no further from this romance of the spirit in the light of electricity than Shakespeare was in the light of a tallow lamp or Homer reciting under the light of stars; for in what day of man did not some modern voice proclaim that belief in any powers outside his own ken was impossible?

"Hear the voice of the Bard!" Blake commands: *"Whose ears*

have heard | The Holy Word | That walk'd among the ancient trees. . . ." My earlier work—*Heavenly City, Earthly City, Medieval Scenes,* or *The Venice Poem*—I had viewed as I wrote as forms embodying or expressing the content of an inner psychological drama; and though, in fact, in the rapture of writing what I experienced was also a world of the poem, where I actually saw in the mind's light persons and knew their lives—Orpheus, the Gnostic Dragon, or the Child Zagreus—in all the force of the real, I thought of them as belonging to the order of symbols relating to the state of my own soul. But, with the book *Letters,* a book that might have been dedicated to Helen Adam, bringing the book of Blake forward to me—for it was by Blake that I read the Zohar in those years—

> O Earth, O Earth, return!
> Arise from out the dewy grass;
> Night is worn
> And the morn
> Rises from the slumberous mass.

—I was already a convert to the Romantic spirit, and myth in that spirit is not only a story that expresses the soul but a story that awakens the soul to the real persons of its romance, in which the actual and the spiritual are revealed, one in the other.

II

Working on this paper, I had prepared for months—the first notes began in June and here I was in the second week of September at this point—not fruitlessly nor along the wrong track, but along tracks that would belong but did not yet belong to what I wanted; gathering the matter in which the spirit of forms did not yet move. The voice, I felt, was not yet in the words, or I couldn't hear it. Nowhere in what I was doing did I feel right about the thing having begun, everywhere it was about to begin; I did not have the "opening" words. For the essay must move, I knew, as the poem moves, from the releasing pattern of an inspiration, a breathing. Facts or ideas or images are not true for me until in them I begin to feel the patterning they are true to, the melody they belong to. Once this feeling of a patterning begins, the work comes to ones hand; the form of the whole can be felt emerging in the fittingness of each passage. I am no longer thinking or proposing ideas but working *with* them, seeing with them, as I work.

They came, the words that keyed in the work of this paper, not in my own writing, but in an early poem of Denise Levertov's which she had interpreted in her essay on Myth for the same conference. Syrinx, *"in fear from unimaginable sound,"* flees from the sound of Pan's lustful pursuit—his thudding hooves, his wild words yet to be growled in her ears. But she is herself, in flight, changed into the first instrument of the very sound she feared—Pan's music. And just there, the lines from the poem appeared which struck the spark or key-note I needed:

> From darkness rose the vibrant grass, the first
> step in a world of flowers, bees, bright birds . . .

From which I took my directive. I too must go back, as I knew from the beginning I must, to childhood, where the germinal experience of poetry and myth lay. I had balked, for I felt I had done all that and too much of that in the H.D. book. Now I was given the lead, the "authority", by another poet, and I followed. It is characteristic of the mythological mind that it takes from perhaps personal expressions of other men and from their works and dreams the commanding authority of an inspired gospel. The Christian Dante will be guided not only by Beatrice, who may be, as Henri Corbin argues in his *Avicenna,* an angelic power, the Active Intelligence, but he will be guided also by the authority of the poet Virgil.

"And then whenever I was feverish and had my temperature taken," the notebook continues, where we left off with the rectangular pond and its following fountain, "there was *Froggy-Would-A-Wooing-Go* to time it. Or there was *I Went to the Animal Fair.* My mother's voice singing or crooning in a humming sound hovers above or around and passes into a silence of concentration which it becomes or survives, in which I work. The Wedding to come or the Ark of Animal Forms that upon the Flood between the one evolutionary epoch and the next carries into survival the species of our present world ecology stirred old myths in dream in my infantile mind.

In the excitement of the poem everything gathers about a point that we discover radiates from our earliest years. The Coda of *The Venice Poem* brought me to a baby's concentration in delite upon a star-sapphire pendant that was, whatever in memory of some past event it might have been, in the time of the poem the birth of a focus in me. The pattern of rime itself is the pattern of this life-resonance, the rebirth of a sound. Erudite, I have been called by some, and even, by others, pretentious, for my studious mythologies, but in every seeming learning search I have but sought among things that belong to my unlearned years.

When, in the poem *Fire,* Bosch's Christ, out of the hell of the seventeenth-century religious wars into the hell of our own century's wars between Capitalist and Communist, appeared —later I would find Him in the actual Christ of the Cao Daï cult in Viet Nam—surrounded by the faces of contemporary public men of our Permanent War Economy, the very faces Bosch painted, gloating, leering or piously grimacing, protesting their love of order as they preside over the violation of

Asia, these were earlier faces I had seen, long before I saw Bosch. Bosch's painting was a rime. And against their evil, the ever-returning scene of brutality and will, I raised a scene of early childhood, a dawn-of-man scene, with its play of leaf-boats and sand harbors in a mountain stream, close and cool with shadow and sunlight, that barely holds. Moments of a childhood are created as Edens, the mythic seed of a power in the story to come. Reinforcing the ideogram of a childhood memory, or *screen* as Freud would have called it, of the peaceable kingdom, in *Chords*, the following poem, I turned to evoke cosmic powers from the oldest myths as they appear in the Orphic theogonies, to bring into the immediate reality, where the political powers at war seem all powerful, awareness of or the presence of the very numen of the Universe.

The word *numen* I take from Rudolf Otto's *The Idea of the Holy*. The numinous is felt as the presence—it *is* the presence —of an overwhelming power of a stone, of a snake, of a man, of a fate, of a word, so that it becomes personal. The numen of the universe is its awful and overwhelming reality as an entity, its *genius*. I do not think lightly of the Creator. I would use a distant and possibly abstract term, "the Creative Will." But the feeling of presence, not concept, remains. The Numen Itself shakes the very language, the words I hope might be no more than words. Speaking of a thing I call upon its name, and the Name takes over from me the story I would tell, if I let the dimmest realization of that power enter here. But the myth we are telling is the myth of the power of the Word. The Word, as we refer to It, undoes all the bounds of semantics we would draw in Its creative need to realize Its true Self. It takes over. Its desire would take over and seem to put out or to drown the individual reality—lonely invisible and consumed flame in the roaring light of the Sun—but Its creativity moves in all the realities and can only realize Itself in the Flesh, in the incarnation of concrete and mortal Form.

[45]

Yet now, when I turn to consult my Latin dictionary I find, yes, *numen* is *the divine will, the will or power of the gods,* and it is also used *"of the* manes *of a beloved person"*; but the first definition given is: *a nodding with the head, a nod.*

It is sleep that overwhelms us, *"our little Death from which we daily | do survive"*, and dream that brings us visions there, as poetry brings vision in our wakeful hours. Myths seem most like dreams, like what Jungians call "big dreams"; just as the Freudian dreams seem to Jung to be "little" or merely personal in their message, and are like the despised folktale. The art of poetry, our craft of reoccurring sounds and themes that give measure and gathering resonances that give depth, of shifting rhythms and dancing numbers, may be the art of a hypnagogic fascination—the attentive head suspended in the middle of a nod.

But it was, when I look closely now, what I began to suspect as I let this idea of the sleepy nodding of a head nod in my head for several days—it was the nod of command that was meant. The verb νεύω in Greek means to nod or *beckon,* as a sign. In our word *nod* as in my thought here the two come together, the sign given by the imperial will and the other, the involuntary nod: "to be momentarily inattentive or inaccurate"; my O.E.D. tells me—"to make a slip or mistake." I do not believe in a Creation by Chance or by Predestined Form but in a Creation by a Creative Will that realizes Itself in Form evolving in the play of primordial patterns. And in my work I evolve the form of a poem by an insistent attention to what happens in inattentions, a care for inaccuracies; for I strive in the poem not to make some imitation of a model experience but to go deeper and deeper into the experience of the process of the poem itself.

When I looked up the word *Myth* in the index of Cook's *Zeus,* Volume III, I found:

Myths arising from art forms misunderstood, arising from facts misunderstood, arising from historical events, arising from literary allusions misunderstood, arising from metaphor, giving rise to would-be history, of accommodation . . .

The poet is not only a maker in the sense of the maker of the poem, but he makes up his mind, he makes up a world within a world, a setting of elements into play, that carries over into a maturity the make-believe of childhood, where, too, certain misunderstandings and mistakes led not to disaster but to fruitful pastures. It is a lesson learned again in Freud's insights that we have not to avoid our misunderstandings but to understand them. For the poet, the fortunate misunderstanding of or mistaking of or forging of the Hebrew word *alma* in Isaiah so that it appears in Greek as *parthenos* to mean Virgin, is an inspired change in the genetic information of the Old Testament. The shadow of the Old Testament becomes the light of the New, Jung shadowly observes. What emerges is a mythic possibility; it is also creative, a poetic structure in our history then. In the actual history of Christian churches it has been a terrible misunderstanding; one has only to think of the bloody and merciless inhumanity in which the actual life of Christian poetry as active dogma has been written. The image of the Virgin is also the Iron Maiden. And where we would take seriously as ours the mistake, and understand the creative misunderstanding, the burning bodies and tortured lives of Jews and heretics must be taken into the full configuration.

What was "accommodation" as a source of myth? Turning to the reference in Cook, I find the following which I would bring into play here:

The fact is, the myth represented in the pediment was a myth of accommodation. At this vital focus of Athenian worship allowance had to be made for the racial and religious changes through which the worshippers had passed. If the results of our somewhat scattered enquiry may be gathered up in the form of a diagram, I should maintain that the cults of the Akropolis can be arranged chronologically in a threefold stratification . . .

He is speaking here of the virgin birth of Athena, and in a footnote he illustrates the account by a passage from Rose's *Handbook of Greek Mythology:*

The close connexion between Zeus and Athena is probably due to historical causes. The chief god of the invaders must come to some sort of terms with the powerful and well-established Minoan-Mycenean goddess; but he cannot be her husband, since she, like the rest of her kind, has either no consort or an insignificant one; therefore he must be her father. But she can have no mother, for that would subordinate her to some other goddess, such as Hera or Persephone, and she is far too important for that. Hence her miraculous birth, which represents, if we could but recover the details, an interesting chapter in early diplomacy and ecclesiastical policy.

This is the historical Athena; and the historical Christ is so written and drawn in layer after layer of historical event. These are layers of a creation or poetry in time. The fundamentalist strives to go back to some authentic *apostolic* Christ which he must create anew in his own light, as the reader seeking to locate the Word, even turning to the dictionary to restrain the newly creative will of his reading, arrives at apostolic meaning; as Jane Harrison or Francis Cornford strive to go back to an authentic ritual from which the Myth flows, or the righteous Communist strives for a pure Leninism or a pure Marxism; but all such resurrections are impure, for they are informed by the creative imagination and the sense of realities of the resurrectionist. Myth gives life-form, and men living in that myth live in its history, in its living changes and permutations, not its petrifactions. Turn back the pages as they will, every part of man's story has been re-informed by the creative genius of his own present moment.

The view that those working in Bible criticism often have that they are disproving the historicity of Jesus as they lay bare the record of complicated forces—inheritances, crossbreedings, misunderstandings, slips of the tongue, mutations—at work in that identity is mistaken; but we must remember too that now all the disproof of Jesus and the disbelief in the Christ Who proclaims Himself to be the primal Love, Light, and Life of Creation enters the living drama of that poetic entity. The heightened sense of myth versus history charges the poem with a moving counterpoint between what we see and what we do not see.

There are those who are dismayed at the analysis of poems, and fundamentalist poets strive to keep their innocence or to rescue from the contamination of knowledge the very firstness and pureness of Poetry's purpose, free from the distortions of "diplomatic and ecclesiastical policy", from all the tarnish of language's associations. Think of the changes time has wrought, and men's imaginations, in the historical body of our reading of the *Iliad*. Each generation has the inspiration, as it gives birth to its own reading, that at last the poem has been cleared of the contamination of false readings and translations and reconceived in the terms of the original authenticity. Recently, attacking the poet Robin Blaser's translation of the *Chimères* of Gérard de Nerval, I struggled myself to restore what I felt was the original intention of Nerval, but I knew too that every alteration in Nerval's text Blaser had made was not to be taken as simply mistranslating or misunderstanding: when we are concerned with Poetry, we are faced, as men in religion are faced, with violent operations of words. A mistake is a mutation altering the life of the spirit.

Blaser had realized a poem of his own, but he had done violence to the text.

So Plato, Herodotus, and Euripides tell us Homer did violence to the myth of Helen and lied in the *Iliad* to suit his own ends. For this he was "blinded", blinded by his art, as was Stesichorus, who was stricken with a disease of the eyes in the divine wrath of Helen and wrote then his *Palinôdia: "That tale was never true! Thy foot never stepped on the benched galley, nor crossed to the towers of Troy,"* and recovered his sight of things. Canto-recanto, the very genius, the creative will of the poem, alters what it would conserve. The creative experience of Man is a Word in its Mutations barely overheard in generation after generation, lost into Itself in Its being found. In this force of confusions, the mythological poet, as distinguished from the personal poet, struggles to keep the original and to relegate all invention to the adversary of the poem: he struggles against the invention that moves him.

By the time "Homer" was written down—and only under the fortune of a tyrant's will did the Greek epic poets give in to the modernism of literacy—by the time that cataclysmic change over from the poet as Mnemosyne's mouthpiece to the poet as Mercury's scribbler took place, generations of reciters and makers had participated in the person of Homer. Now, as readers of the text, not rememberers of the text, it is in our readings that the life, that is, the development and enduring presence, continues. And, given the actual existence of the "original", with a different conscience translators take over; for their alterations do not alter their model. Memory must strive to preserve to the letter; but Writing preserves in itself the first version, and we see the more clearly how our very reading varies from reader to reader, from generation to generation. The morphology of forms, in evolving, does not destroy their historicity but reveals that each event has its origin in the origin of all events; yes, but in turn, we are but the more aware that the first version is revised in our very turning to it, seeing it with new eyes. And in the ecology of forms we begin to see, as we have held in faith, the fittingness, the tellingness of events—their truth—lies in their belonging to the evolution of forms. They cannot *not* belong. Our responsibility as artists is to recognize as fully and as deeply as we can what that be-longingness consists of; to quicken our responses in what we are doing in the poem.

If I take the truth of things to be the truth of their belong-ing to this form of forms, having its completion in the end of time and space, surely beyond my individual comprehension, in my poetics I let go of striving to claim some authenticity for the poem in itself and give its authority over into a universal authenticity that arises from the store of human experience acknowledged in the language that gives whatever depth to my own experience, a feel of form acknowledged in its incep-tion to be no more than a feel. "*I get the drift I do not | know. The Word moves me.*" What seems to the gnostic to be a very gnosis, is an error if it is more than such a feel of the universe, the register of an intense locus of in-formation in man's own formations. It is not that I take the nature of man, my own nature, to be written in a secret key, but that, believing all of Creation to be in process an evolution and revelation of Itself, and the meaning of the parts, the meaning of all definitions, to be posited finally in a totality of resonances, I hold too that the meaning and form of any poem is momentous, yes; but has its motive beyond the conscious and personal intent or realization of the poet. My poetry has, as my individual body has, its own interior systematic structure regardless of "me". I may be expressive in my bodily gestures, I may steer a course of health with care; but its true system lies in "the great house-hold", as I call it in the poem "Orders:"

[51]

There is no
good a man has in his own things except
it be in the community of every thing;
no nature he has
but in his nature hidden in the heart of the living,
in the great household.
The cosmos will not
dissolve its orders at man's evil.

The dialectic of this Sentence in which every happening informs all other parts of the structure appears in history as a
poetry of events. As the proclamation of Love shook the Hellenistic world—and it is not only in the Identity of Christ as
Light, Life and Love that this information acts—having its
locus there, given its locus there, the resonance of Love as a
command and judgment upon history works its changes
throughout a field of Man. Christ Himself and the Father
stand tested in the light and life of Love. As Christ is an eternal
person of God, we read that Love, Brotherhood, is throughout Creation the formative Will. In the end of times, this it is
that is happening. The Earth travails toward the truth of Itself in Love. The primal Eros of Hesiod's *Theogony* climbs upon the Cross, where He is the monster-husband Who comes
to Psyche in the dark of her wish palace.

In the shock of the command, the Christian church as we
first see it in history has retracted the identity of the brother
they are to love to the true believer, or they have translated
Love to mean conversion or even ruthless persecution and
damnation in order to save the enemy from his own iniquity.
The broader community of Christians, even as they preserve
the humanity of their God, come to despise the human body
and the human world about them. Plotinus will be outraged
by the hatred that Gnostics and Christians alike exhibit toward the Cosmos. St. Augustine preserves in his conversion

from the religion of Mani to Christianity the underlying ab-horrence of the Flesh. In the retraction of sympathies before the unbearable declaration of universal sympathies, Christians are soon not only condemning and burning where they were once condemned and burned, but they take their way now in a righteousness that despises the living body—What had been the kerygma of the Incarnation, if not the divine nature of our mortality?—and the cosmos, which no longer appeared as a divine order but as a fallen and corrupted world belonging to Satan.

"The fiction of men, composed with an evil intention," the Christian doctrines seem to the Emperor Julian: "They despise the divinity at work in animals and plants, and even in the Sun Himself." But, if Christians despised the divine nature of the Sun, Julian in turn despises the emerging humanity of the folktale or fairytale Jesus and the lowliness of His disciples. Sounding like the status-conscious critic of Denise Levertov's humble household spirits, the Emperor Julian is scornful of the fact that Christianity appeals to contemptible men, "such as innkeepers, publicans, dancers, and others of the like!", and scornful too of the inglorious and plebian, even slavish, character of the Jesus story:

> But Jesus, who made converts of the worst part of you, has been celebrated by you for little more than three hundred years. And performed during the whole time that he lived no deed which deserves to be mentioned, unless one fancies that to cure the blind and the lame, and to exorcise those possessed by daemons, in the villages of Bethsaida, and Bethania, rank among the greatest undertakings.

Soon Christ was to take over the full trappings of Sol Invictus, the paraphernalia of the Imperator Mundi, even as He took over the birthday of the Solar Mithra. The Son was to be the Sun. And if Jesus had announced that his Kingdom was not of this world; in this worldly time and space, in the Byzantine and Roman empires, Emperor and Pope come to claim a plenitude of power in His Name, a vicarious Will in which Caesar and Christ assume a single Identity. It seems little to have been the Power of Love. Certainly, it appeared and still appears today, more in the likeness of the overweening pride of Julian than in the clothes of the humble and even despised Jesus in His passion.

In the very swelling hour of the Satanic vanity of Popes, their righteousness feeding like a tick upon the blood of heretical martyrs, a very voice of Love was to be heard at the heart of the Catholic world, as if, for the moment, in a fresh bloom, the Love of the Cosmos and the Love of Brothers might be united in one body. *"Be praised, Lord, with all your creatures, | and especially our brother sun,"* Saint Francis sings in his Canticle.

He seemed to those who followed the poetic prophecies of the Abbot Joachim de Flora to be the herald of or even the genius of the New Age of the Holy Spirit that would follow the Age of the Son's Suffering and the Age of the Father's Wrath. The mythical history of religion and poetry were joined in him; for it seemed too as if the Spirit of Romance that once had flourished among the heretics of Provence now laid waste by crusade—it seemed as if the Spirit of Romance had taken root in the Church itself. Francis was declared a saint in his lifetime, an adroit move of ecclesiastical polity; but those who obeyed in faith his Last Testament were declared heretical and burned within a decade of his death. Like the figure of Jesus, the figure of Francis comes to us from canonical and uncanonical story, appearing in a configuration of orthodox and heretical accounts.

Again, in the sixteenth century, another saint who is also a poet appears—Saint John of the Cross. And, after reading Rene Fülöp-Miller's study of the Jesuits, I would add Ignatius

Loyola, who revives in a living theatrical poetry the very Jesus, companion of the outcast and the destitute, the diseased and the mentally-ill, that the Emperor Julian had raised to men's scorn. The little band of the Society of Jesus seems very like the despised Love communities that appear today among the growing number of the disowned that we call hippies: "They went about in rags, and lived in dilapidated houses without doors or windows, in which they were exposed to malaria mosquitoes. They starved, begged, and distributed the money they obtained in this way . . ."

Romance and Poetry haunt this world-as-theater in which the acting company of Jesus in the exercise of Christ's passion will undergo transformation after transformation. The Franciscans, established as an order, will no longer follow Francis' command to serve the Lady Poverty and to make humble, even to humiliate, the mind, but will become one of the wealthiest orders in Europe, and from their ranks will come the most arrogant mountain of intellectual system in all philosophy. The Society of Jesus, from the dramatically inspired group of college drop-outs, staging their Christian happenings, will produce in time those school masters we find in Joyce's *Portrait of the Artist as a Young Man*. But, important to us, who are concerned with the role myth and poetry play in the emerging sense of our universal humanity, the transition from the closed systems of canonical or national traditions to the mixing-ground of man's commonality in myth, must be the work of Jesuits in the seventeenth and eighteenth centuries, where, in China, Christianity was grafted to the Tao and the cult of ancestors in arch diplomacies and a profusion of astronomical and mechanical marvels to set the stage; or, in Paraguay, where Christianity is wed to the tribal innocence of the Indians in a musical and communistic Utopia, a Kingdom of the Sun, "even full orchestras, which included 'violins, contrabasses, clarinets, flutes, harps, trumpets, horns and tympani'", or, in Europe, where the magic lantern of Father Athanasius Kircher projects ancient Egyptian hieroglyphs in the light of their Christian spectacles.

Fülöp-Miller writes in discussing the Jesuit theater: "There were trap-doors for ghost apparitions and vanishing acts, flying machines and cloud apparatus. On every conceivable occasion, the Jesuit producers made divinities appear in the clouds, ghosts rise up and eagles fly over the heavens . . ." And he quotes from a record in the archives of the town of Görz:

> First the crafty Odysseus crossed the stage in a ship . . . Then the astonished crowd saw and heard Orpheus, the gentle conqueror of wild beasts and stones, who sang so sweetly beyond expectation to the lyre that beasts, rocks and pillars moved and followed his melody. This was so cunningly contrived that many stupid people thought that the animals, rocks and pillars had actually become living things . . .

The Jesuit pageants will give rise to the great Romantic theater of Mozart's Masonic mystery-play, *The Magic Flute*, and the mythological splendors of the Faustian theater— Goethe's *Faust* itself, Wagner's *Ring*, and Ibsen's *Peer Gynt*.

In her essay "The Guest", contained in the book *By Avon River*, H.D. traces through the transmission of the cult of Love, from the scattered remnants of the heretical Provencal church, by troubador and romancier, and from the Roman Catholic church, after the looting of the chapels under Henry the Eighth:

> We are apt to forget that many of the original masques and plays were acted in the palace itself, in the throne-room or in the ante-chamber. The decor, the decorations, the ornate imported mirrors, the purple hangings, the dais steps, the embroidered tapestry were all there. Why is this forgotten? The plays of Shakespeare had scenery waiting for them. Portia's caskets are produced

by the Lord Treasurer, perhaps they are alms boxes from some magnificent cathedral. For the Capulet banquet, the scene is already laid. The musicians have only to tune up, in the gallery. Sumptuous plate and linen, looted from the Cardinal's palace, was shared alike by Montague and Capulet. Juliet's tomb was, no doubt, magnificently draped in violet. The candle-sticks recalled another canopy, another burial. The church was plundered by the palace; the palace became the background for a new ritual.

"Into the great vacuum, left by the flame that had hung alike over Catholic and Protestant martyr," she continues, "there rushed with the whirlwind of the Pentecost, this host, drunk with new wine." In the mixing ground of the Hellenistic world, the very kerygma of the second Eros, Love, had entered our historical responsibility. And the first Eros—the wrathful, jealous, revengeful Eros of the Old Testament is called into question, Strife Himself, that Heraclitus called Father of All, taken now in the incarnation of the Son to be Loving. Following the expropriation of the Church in England, the things of the cathedral pass over to become things of the stage, and the creative idea of Love passes from the alembic of the community of saints to the alembic of a community of lovers. Forbidden Romanish things, carrying with them for the imagination the story of Love to whom they belonged, became properties of a stage where the drama was not "Catholic" or "Christian" but in the reawakening of the old world in the new the beginning of a human drama, an illusion in which all mankind's experience was taken as the true ground of human reality, Catholic and heretic reconciled as, after the death of Romeo and Juliet, Capulet and Montague are reconciled through young lovers. In the charm of H.D.'s vision of this history, Richmond's proclamation at the end of *Richard* III, "We will unite the white rose and the red," has double-meaning. The shadows and illuminations of the cathedral now appear in the formation of a tradition in Poetry. Spencer, Marlowe, Shakespeare, are haunted poets compared with the good Chaucer. Dryden will see the giant British genius frozen in ice in his *King Arthur*; and in the rationalist poetics of the following century, things Romanish and Romantic will be exorcised in Calvinist good-sense and business. Poetry will become things oft thought before but ne'er so well expressed.

These saints I picture here, and then the poets, drawing from the Eros of saints, drawing that figure into the complex of another Eros drawn from the Spirit of Romance, are themselves transformed by their imagination of that Eros and then their belonging, as they live in terms of that imagination, to a myth in history in which that Eros has its creative life. Men's visions and fictions as well as their facts move their histories and belong to the reality principle. And facts, what men actually do, are, in the lives of saints like Francis or poets like Dante or Blake, not true in themselves but true in a Poetics whose Poetry is the real world. In turn, Blake, Dante, or Saint Francis, belong here, as I recall them, to my own vision of that poetics, a vision that I have drawn from my readings as well as my personal daily life and from dreams. In this finding, in the active acknowledgment of the finding, that vision is the truth of my readings, life and dreams. To take Blake or Dante as gospels of Poetry, as I do, is to testify to and in that to enter into the reality of a divine history within what men call history.

Time and again, men have chickened out in the fear of what that hawk, the genius of Poetry, threatens, and surrendered their imaginations to the proprieties and rationalizations of new schools of criticism, grammarians, commonsense philosophers, and arbiters of educated best taste. The criticism of modernists like Eliot, Pound, Marianne Moore, Wallace Stevens is hedged about and directed by their sense of what respectable educated opinion is, the tolerance and intolerance of schoolmasters of English Literature and Philosophy the world over. And this tolerance and intolerance has been shaped in turn by the retraction of sympathies, particularly by the retraction of enthusiasm in reaction to the terrible experience the sixteenth and seventeenth centuries knew as men crazed by religious genius fought their civil wars. Augustine in *The City of God* attacks the Old Gods for the cruelties and degradations they have inspired in men; and the history of the inspiration of the New Gods—of the Father, the Son, the Holy Ghost—is written in like holocausts and massacres as well as in upliftings and fulfillings of man's desires. Men have been as corrupted and twisted in their nature by the Christian myth as they have been released into new nature.

When we lament the contraction and even the retraction of sympathies, we must remember that the extension of the area in which we participate emotionally is the extension too of our mythic or story-life; wherever we open ourselves to myth it works to convert us and to enact itself anew in our lives. Every sympathy is the admission of a power over us, a line in which sympathetic magic is at play. In the fullness of our potential sympathetic identification with the world, if the reality of contemporary science is not restricted to an empirical realm but taken to be, in that, spiritual and poetic, that is, creative, we can sicken in signs of the most remote planet or die in the evil intent of an ancestral enemy. In the sympathy which today has with yesterday, the living reality of all times in present time, the feeling of continuous identity in creation, the convert of psychoanalysis may become the victim of a deprivation that actually took place long ago and in another country. The theory of the collective unconscious advanced by Freud gives new life to the meaning of original sin. To inherit or to evolve is to enter mythic existence.

In the tribute poets pay, after Dryden, to deliver over their art to the consensus of reasonable men, poetry, like the universe of rationalist science, ceases to be primal Creation and becomes a commodity, a material for human uses and self-development. Poems will be viewed as competing in the great market of values, even as men compete there, and an evaluative criticism grows up. Self-made men and self-made poems take pride in their rise. The operations of allegory and metaphor cease to be magical and become manners of speaking, displays of wit, and historical events themselves cease to be thought of as informed by a creative intent, to be read as omens and portents, showings forth of meaning within meaning, intent within intent, of a momentous design in which men in their acts participate and to which they contribute, in terms of which men know or do not know their roles. Now wars like business are practical affairs, and the body counts from the battle fields of Viet Nam are issued like the scores of football and baseball teams.

When Milton on November 24, 1644, addresses the Puritan parliament in the *Areopagitica,* he is not illustrating a principle with a figure of speech but recalling to their conscience and consciousness the meaning of what they do as revealed in a myth that is also the true history hidden in history. That Truth here is also Love and the Light, and that it is the Myth itself, the story of what is happening in history that we but know in part, Tobecontinued's Tale, as Joyce calls it in *Finnegan's Wake,* springs from the same certainty as to the principle of things as that in which Christ is proclaimed to be Love, Light and the True Life:

> Truth indeed came once into the world with her divine Master, and was a perfect shape most glorious to look on: but when he ascended, and his Apostles after him were laid asleep, then arose a wicked race of deceivers, who as that story goes of the *Ægyptian Typhon* with his conspirators, how they dealt with the good *Osiris,* took

the Virgin Truth, hewd her lovely form into a thousand peeces, and scatter'd them to the four winds. From that time ever since, the sad friends of Truth, such as durst appear, imitating the carefull search that *Isis* made for the mangl'd body of *Osiris,* went up and down gathering up limb by limb still as they could find them. We have not yet found them all, Lords and Commons, nor ever shall doe, till her Masters second comming; he shall bring together every joynt and member, and shall mould them into an immortall feature of loveliness and perfection . . . The light which we have gain'd, was giv'n us, not to be ever staring on, but by it to discover oneward things more remote from our knowledge.

The mythological mind—and mine, like Milton's here, is mythological—hears this not as fable or parable but as the actual drama or meaning of history, the plot and intention of Reality. The story of Virgin Truth who "came once into the world with her divine Master" and then whose form is torn to pieces would refer in the minds of the Puritan Parliament opportunely, and Milton knew that opportunity, to the rending of Christ's universe of sympathies into a history of strife, a war declared by the established Churches upon heretical cults —"*Ev'n them who kept thy truth so pure of old,*" the poet in his sonnet "On the late Massacher in Piedmont" thinking of the Waldenses might be thinking too of the poet's keeping of truth in Poetry, another line of transmission from the esoteric Eros. Truth was a Power, and, in this, a Person in history. And the Parliament in serving Her would become Her champions and servants; the cult of the Virgin Truth replacing the earlier cult of the Virgin Queen in Spenser's time.

Traditions bearing such a gnosis of not-knowing enter into Milton's concept of the myth of Truth. In philosophy, we think of the agnosticism of Socrates—if I may import to the time of Plato the word that came into existence in our own time in the wake of Darwin's vision of the evolution of Life. Socrates knew he did not know. And with the Romantic movement, the intellectual adventure of not knowing, of "Negative Capability", Keats called it in poetry, returns. The truth we know is not of What Is, but of What Is Happening. In Milton's myth, all of history is a travail, and the Truth of What Is Happening, its What Is, lies only in the second comming, the end of Happening. Christ's life is the immediate historical reality of the Form, or the proclamation of that Form, happening in this poetry of process; and the Second Coming is the Form of Forms from which all Judgment and redemption of events flows. But here again I am speaking of the wholeness of a poem in which all its parts are redeemed as meaning. Creatively, in turn, everything that happens in writing the poem, as it belongs to the poem, must be acknowledged and undertaken as meaning. "Think upon the meaning of this act," is the command of the creative will.

Jungians in their scorn for the lowness of Freud's world of anatomical meanings divide dreams into "big" dreams, Jungian dreams, showing deep images and archetypal content, and "little" dreams, Freudian dreams, reducing the meaning to the interests of lower organs and orders, "such as innkeepers, publicans, dancers, and others of the kind." Jung himself, when his mind is not shadowed by his thought of Freud, will be very wary everywhere else of such divisions into opposites. But the essential difference is that Jung thinks theosophically, where Freud thinks mythologically. In the world of myth, Eros and Thanatos rule in the Creative Will. As in the theogony of Hesiod, Kronos castrates the Father with Earth's knife and throws the penis upon the waves of the sea which becomes the primal Aphrodite. In the philosophy of Plato or the theosophies of Plutarch, Proclus or Jung, the critical mind avoids the lowness of the story and reads in highminded symbols.

In the Form of Forms all events, persons, presentations, stories are redeemed or revealed as form and content; as in the Freudian reading of the dream, all parts belong, no member is to be dismissed as trivial or mistaken. Mistakes themselves mark the insistence of meanings in other meanings; more is present than we would rightly want to take it was present. For Freud, not only dream but waking reality is not meaningless or formless but to be read in signs. The numen commands or beckons from every stone. Men's lies themselves told the truth about them.

The analyst has redeemed as revelation of what he calls the subconscious or the Id all the despised and exploded errors from the dormitories of the soul that men had dismissed as irrational. Now, as in the ancient world, the language of madmen, children, dreams, and of myths, that had been thought unintelligible was shown to yield meaning. If we could tell the literal truth of things uncolored by our own presence in them, we might be masterly liars. But human liars must create their figments of truth, and in so doing betray the very hidden wishes and identities they mean to conceal. Patients who present the analyst with a pseudo-dream, Freud realized, in making up the counterfeit come close upon dreaming. Once making up begins, the fictive process is a poetry; and dreaming, the Romantics had realized, was involuntary Poetry. The grace of the poem, the voice, comes from a will that strives to waken us from our own personal will or to put that will to sleep. Many poets can write only as they dream, if they do not consciously participate in the poem but, avoiding all analytic recognitions, become entranced, Trilbys of the genius of the poem. But that angel of the event of the poem gives the poet both a permission and a challenge. The poet waking from waking takes up the challenge of the voice of the poem and wrestles against sleep, bringing all the watchful craft and learned art into the striving form in order that that much recognition and admission enter into the event. He strives to waken to the will of the poem, even as the poem strives to waken that will.

III

Recalling the Saints who were also Poets—Francis, John of the Cross and Ignatius Loyola, in whose lives a poetry of history itself was created, men who lived in the Christian myth, I had the sense too of how in time in each order an antithesis or antipoetry had appeared in their names, and I set about craftily to sketch out this part of the plot. Just here, the delite in cunning fashioning carried me into the false illustration of the Franciscan anti-type in the invitingly monumental *Summa* of Aquinas, and such was my satisfaction in the juxtaposition of these two, Francis and Saint Thomas, that he *had* to be Franciscan. Only the baffled look of a friend as I read the passage brought me to check myself. But the false note was to remain. In the demonstration of how myth operates in the life and truth of the poet's work contained in this paper as our immediate example of that work, I saw the good of the error. For a time it must jar in the reader's appreciations, and I must incur the being-seen-through, caught in the act of a would-be clever effect.

Often I must force myself to remain responsible to the error that sticks in pride's craw; not to erase it, but to bring it forward, to work with it, even if this flaw mar a hoped-for success. Pound in the *Terminology* of Chinese ideograms for his Confucius translations defines "Sincerity" as: "the sun's lance coming to rest on the precise spot verbally . . . to perfect, bring to focus." Here, what I wanted to bring to focus was finally, as often it is for me in the poem, what is happening in the composition itself: the work of art is itself the field we would render the truth of. Focusing in on the process itself as the field of the poem, the jarring discord must enter the composition.

Another ideogram Pound stresses means: "Fidelity to the given word. The man here standing by his word." This faithfulness, this truth to the word, I take to mean not that the writer deny the possibility of error and defend his statement, but that he face the possibility of error and seek the truth of his statement.

In the aftermath of the War, Pound stands in the full consequences of his Confucian myth of the state compounded with his Renaissance myth of the Prince brought over into his idealization of the tyrant Mussolini, as Petrarch before him had acclaimed the tyrant Cola di Rienzi. In the nineteen-thirties, Canto XLVI had been cautionary:

> And if you will say that this tale teaches . . .
>   a lesson, or that the Reverend Eliot
>   has found a more natural language . . . you who think
>   you will
>   get through hell in a hurry . . .

Now in the Pisan Cantos we find among the properties of the poet's mind and the goods of his experience rescued from Hell, the admission of a serious flaw, "the six seeds of an error"; and in the great Cantos of his old age, the theme grows:

> Tho my errors and wrecks lie about me.
> And I am not a demigod
>   the damn stuff will not cohere?

"*Many errors,* | *a little rightness.*" There are those, and they are many, who believe they have him there, proved less than a poet should be, cut down to size. But Pound is heroic, for he had taken upon himself a commitment to order, as the tragic hero Oedipus took a commitment to a law that condemned him, and he has come into the judgment of that resolve. At Venice in 1964, in despair of his art—the despair that only

[65]

the artist most seriously wrestling for his art to be true knows
—he said in interview: "It's not so, not strictly so. That's the trouble."

Not only Christianity but all Churches that proceed from a revealed Truth, the ground of the one true Life in light of which all human experience is to be judged true or false, saved or damned, awakened or dead asleep, must labor to convert reality to the truth of itself. But in that labor its workers have the faith that theirs is the strait true way, the rest are false. They have received the strict truth, "it is so, strictly so", and have been received into, saved by, the proclamation.

Philosophy must always dwell in the question of things, enamored of wisdom, seek to look into the nature of what is meant by truth itself, how do we feel it, how do we know it. And science assumes that there is something to know but must always—I am thinking here of our contemporary theoretical sciences—be at work in the field of what it does not know, conserving all the facts of what it has come to know in the light of a picture of a total order that it may never come to know; the laws of science are creative pictures then, imagined orders that have their truth posited in physical facts.

For the religious mind, all human experience and facts of the universe that do not conform to the strait truth are false experience, either ignorant of their own true nature or dishonest about that nature. The truth religion knows has no deceit in it but casts such a light that we see a world filled with deceit.

For the poet, *It,* the form he obeys in making form, the very revelation of Art, is not strictly so. Creativity, as I have suggested, means such a change in the meanings of every part in the creation of each part that every new strictness is also a charm undoing all previous strictnesses, at once an imperative and at the same time a change of imperative. Each syllable of the poem, if we keep alive each sound in the sounding of the whole, is such a stricture—just the sound it is—that proves in the movement of the poem to be a liberation. But let us take just this concrete immediacy of the poem: I start with the word "Father", and since I compose by the tone-leading of vowels, the vowels are notes of a scale, in which breaths move, but these soundings of spirit upon which the form of the poem depends are not constant. They are the least lasting sounds in our language; even in my lifetime, the sound of my vowels alters. There is no strict vowel standard.

Then in the very radical meaning of the word poetry, *poiein* to make, we rightly suspect there is present all the artfulness in the art, craftiness in the craft, the cunning to make fit— "Sleight-of-soul" I called it in *Medieval Scenes* where I wanted to project the mistrust of reality that informs the gnostic vision of the world. But I do not mistrust reality any more than I trust it: I seek it with an ardor that leads as it misleads. If *poiein*, the concept of the poet fashioning the poem, making a world of the poem, enters into my poetics, and it does; so also does the Celtic idea of the poet as bard, the chant that enchants, the myth or tale as *spell* and words that cast images upon the mind—here Christ fulfilling the law of the Old Testament is seen as living in its spell; and with this Germanic or Celtic strand from the pagan woods of the North, and the Greek strand from the artisans' studios of the South, I combine in one rope of my art the third Jewish strand, where song comes to David's lips, not fashioned, but as the voice moves him. The universalism of this art precludes its being strictly so.

"We are such stuff," the wisdom of the poet-as-magician in *The Tempest* proclaims: "as dreams are made of." In Poetry as in Dream, the man in search of the truth of things must distinguish between the Gate of the Horns, dream sent by ancestral ghosts, and the Gate of gleaming Ivory, the cloud- *like sky* gates of Heaven, wherefrom come not only true but false dreams or deceitful dreams. In the *Iliad,* Zeus sends a dream simulacre of Nestor to Agamemnon to urge him to return to Greece; and Apollo fashions an eidolon of Æneas to confound the Greeks. As, from Euripides we learn, the Helen of Troy was such a false dream. Speaking in the language of actual things derived from our familiar lives, the gods convey cunningly duplicit messages.

Before Hesiod calls upon the Muses—and not only the muses of Poetry but the muse of History is among them—to tell him his *Theogony,* Hesiod tells us that when first they taught him glorious song, they declared: "We know how to speak many false things as though they were true; but we know, when we will, to utter true things."

Myth then, coming from the knowledge only the daughters of Memory have of First Things, comes with all the risk of truth we still preserve in our daily speech when we speak of something being no more than "a story," "a myth," "poetry."

The Divine Will in Poetry is Creative, and its inspiration is never single-minded or strait, but creates a field of meanings. Yet, like the strait way of truth in which the man of religion is sure, the actual realized poem is just the one form that it is: to write at all is to come into a sentence; make that sentence however I will, cut it short before it is started or weave it as if endlessly, how I actually do make that sentence is the strait and narrow identity of just these decisions. In man's hands all free councils become fateful, as in the poet's hands the free movements potential in language lead into poetic conclusions. The straitness or strictness of making we experience as the inevitability of the poem; and in turn the straitness or strictness of even the most universalizing mind imprints upon its works a style, a cruelty, a making us see and feel in this unique personal way.

In the Homeric *Hymn to Hermes,* the Child-God finding a tortoise laughs out and says: "Living, you shall be a spell against mischievous witchcraft; but if you die, then you shall make beautiful song"—"*And though it has been said,*" Shelley translates:

> That you alive defend from magic power,
> I know you will sing sweetly when you're dead.

From the body of what alive gave an immunity to magic, the infant magician, scooping out the shell, makes the magic of the lyre—"pondering sheer trickery in his heart—deeds such as knavish folk pursue in the dark night-time."

Stealing the Oxen of the Sun, as poets would steal a march upon truth and loot the treasuries of the Gods, and hiding his ways in artful invention, this new God of Poets designs his own myth to bewilder Apollo, the God of Poetries. If the God of the religious man speaks the strict truth; the poet's God twists the truth so that it seems other than it is. "I too will enter upon the rite Apollo has," Hermes tells his mother: "If my father will not give it me, I will seek—and I am able— to be a prince of robbers."

Step by step we can read the duplicities and cunning protestations the poet keeps before the power of poetry. He is but a child. When Apollo lifts him up and starts to carry him in his arms to go to Zeus, Hermes farts, "an omen, a hand-worked belly-serf, a rude messenger," and sneezes to cover, whereupon Apollo drops him. The high and the low interplay bewilderingly.

He is the son of Maia, a goddess who lives in a deep cave. She may be the genius of Plato's Cave, the great Māyā or Illusion of Hindu mythology. And her son, Hermes, is the genius of invention. He not only invents the bow and the lyre, but fire and fictions, or truths so invented that they are unbelievable. One of the sources of invention is the disguise of what is so. And though this *Hymn to Hermes* is comic, as all myths of the Trickster are, beneath the comic there is a sinister possibility. Where there is always more than is apparent, the comic is an uneasy mask. There is trickery in the very nature of creation itself; innovation can only come from what we do not know. We might recall here the emerging picture of the evolution of life in our contemporary cosmic myth, where freakish mutations excited by cosmic radiations from the sun and other stars enter into the creation of new species. Man is most uneasy and hence humorous about the playfulness of his creativity.

From the beginning, seeing through his experience, undoing as well as doing, cynicism as well as creative myth, have been necessary to keep alive the wholeness of man's experience and sanity. "Poetry," Ezra Pound in the late 1940's sent out the instruction in a postcard from St. Elizabeth's Hospital, "is to debunk by lucidity." The sun is no bigger than we see it is, the sensory debunker will declare, to counter in some way his apprehension of the powers and overwhelming reality of the sun. We protect our boundaries, the very shape of what we are, by closing our minds to the truth, remain true to what we are. And man's mind itself has moods when it would take refuge in being no bigger than and no more than the brain in his skull; and again, his mind has only those limits that his imagination of the universe itself has.

Each man in his seriousness is concerned, deeply concerned, to live in the truth of things. The man of religion to whom the truth has been revealed; the man of philosophy for whom the nature of the truth must ever be sought out and tried; the man of science for whom the truth of things is a lure in the universe exciting him to search and to make ever new imaginative pictures as the truth he cannot reach requires—how difficult it is for these serious men to believe in or respect or understand sympathetically the seriousness of the others. At heart each is like a cuckolded lover, who sees his beloved Truth at once violated and that, insincerely, by his rival.

The man of religion must see the world in terms of what he can believe and not believe. The philosopher sees it in terms of what he can question and cannot question, belief does not enter his experience. Indeed, philosophy, like poetry, stops in its tracks where belief or disbelief enters in. The scientist sees the seriousness of reality not in the terms of belief or question, but in the terms of what he can test and prove to relate to some order of the world.

How out of it all the creative artist must seem, where he plays with belief and disbelief, absorbed in serious fictions, "imitations" of what other men really feel and think; even giving himself up wholly to such fancies. For there is no art except a man die. In poetry, as in religion, philosophy, science . . . but these are only three of man's many other life realities; as in politics, in industry, in household, in wandering —we come to no life unless we are ready to die utterly to let life take over. We work as poets and take seriously what seems to most men the one ground surely not to be taken seriously— the play-reality of imagined religions, philosophies, sciences. We have been converted by and have now taken our faith in a truth that is patently made-up. The poet who thunders with the voice of God speaks from a reality that is not only inspired but has to be realized in terms in which the craft and wishes of the man are thoroughly complicit. Here, in what seems to men the most obviously tricky of all realms, "beside himself", the poet can become a shape-shifter so that we know not who he is. Think of the creative insincerity of Shakespeare who appears in all the dramatis personae of his plays as most genuinely Hamlet or Lady Macbeth, except that "I" of the sonnets that men cannot believe for sure, so that Shakespeare will always appear to be actually someone else—Bacon or Queen Elizabeth; or, the poet speaking in the person of animals, elements, worlds, all Time—where Dame Mutability may have Her speech and is more real to us than Spenser, and Beatrice give

[71]

counsel in musical rime. The poet is not master of reality but its lover; and falling in love, charmed by reality, returns in the midst of that charm to fulfill the law of the poem itself. Only in the poem as he actually makes it will the Poetry that moves him come into existence.

The greatest poets—for me, two, beyond all others, stand: Dante and Shakespeare—especially, the greatest poets, must ever be troubled by the play of their genius, of true things in fictions, and of fictions in true things. Here, let me take, as an example of how uneasy the truth of mythical reality in poetry must be, Dante's careful accounting for the nature of the angel Amor as He appeared in the course of the poet's *Vita Nuova:*

Dante would justify the poetic eidolon of the Sonnet that begins (in Rossetti's translation):

> I felt a spirit of Love begin to stir
>   Within my heart, long time unfelt till then;
>   And saw Love coming towards me, fair and fain,
> (That I scarce knew him for his joyful cheer)
> Saying, "Be now indeed my worshipper!"
>   And in his speech he laugh'd and laugh'd again.

That Dante is not illustrating some thought of his but telling us of an actual presentation is the crux of the reality of the poem; and, certainly, it would be difficult to argue that this angel Amor is the Christ as Love. In any event, this is not what Dante does. Since the presentation appears in the excitement of poetic reverie, Dante pleads *poetic license,* that this is no more than a figure of speech. This is not simply a matter of literary definitions, but we are aware that, as he marshals every resource to answer, he is answering to the prescriptions of a philosophy that has consequences in theological courts.

"I have spoken of Love as though it were a thing outward and visible: not only a spiritual essence but as a bodily substance also." He certainly had! In the beginning of the *Vita Nuova* he tells us of another visitation of the angel: "And betaking me to the loneliness of mine own room, I fell to thinking of this most courteous lady, thinking of whom I was overtaken by a pleasant slumber, wherein a marvellous vision was presented to me: for there appeared to be in my room a mist of the color of fire, within the which I discerned the figure of a lord of terrible aspect." This Visitation, that Dante raises in our minds in the glamor of poetry as He had come to the poet in the phantasy of dream, is not a figure of speech, and yet He is related to true figures of speech; actual seeings excited by the hallucinogenic powers of words, beings who answer a spell. "The which thing, in absolute truth, is a fallacy; Love not being of itself a substance, but an accident of substance," Dante recants.

Dante pleads the excuse of poetic license: "In Horace man is made to speak to his own intelligence as unto another person (and not only hath Horace done this, but herein he followeth the excellent Homer) . . . Through Ovid, Love speaketh as a human creature . . . neither did these ancient poets speak thus without consideration, nor should they who are makers of rhyme in our day write after the same fashion, having no reason in what they write; for it were a shameful thing if one should rhyme under the semblance of metaphor or rhetorical similitude, and afterwards, being questioned thereof, should be unable to rid his words of such semblance, unto their right understanding. Of whom (to wit, of such as rhyme thus foolishly) myself and the first among my friends do know many."

This satisfaction of right understanding is counter to the mode of Dante's poetry, which is not that of a romance about imaginary beings but of a testimony of visionary experience. The poem insists upon the primal reality of the angel Amor, of Beatrice, of Virgil; and all the polysemous meanings of these persons are also, if the poem be not trival, polysemous mean-

[73]

ings revealed in the poet's actual life. Homer tells about Troy; and Ovid recounts the lives of the Gods; they are story-tellers and not autobiographers, and both we and the early Greeks saw them that way. But Dante here, in the daring of his *Comedy,* if he be taken as sincere, being himself the hero or protagonist of his poem, raises all the trouble the active imagination raises when it invades the testimony of the actual. Joan will be tried by ecclesiastic court and burned at the stake for talking with such demonic powers as Dante's angels in the *Vita Nuova* are. And, after Gemisthos Plethon brings the cult of the old gods into intellectual Italian circles, Ficino and Pico della Mirandola will come into trial for their practices of a theurgic magic to call up such personifications. Remembering such cases, we may see the poet's defense in a new light. Dante, by pleading the insincerity of just what in the poem has to be sincere, secured for the poet a special dispensation at the cost of a semantic twist in which vision became conceit and angelic visitation no more than a fancy way of speaking.

This is double-speak, the truth that only those who know the truth can penetrate. He confesses even as he dismisses the charge. Our cunning Hermes laughs in the risibility of the Angel, as Dante in the recantation of his fallacies lists: "And secondly, I say that Love smiled; and thirdly, that Love spake; faculties (and especially the risible faculty) which appear proper unto man." A sense of the humor at play in human experience to keep alive the equilibrations of a sanity when the divine comes into play. But Dante in this seemingly disarming and rationalizing passage has given us also the inheritance of grammatical magic, constructs of poetic idea more potent than opium to enchant, than psychedelic drugs to activate the primary imagination. Every "fallacy" is a verity of the poetic experience. In a Christian world, where Christ is not only Man and God, but Love and Logos, words are, like men themselves, fields of Life.

[74]

Christ, who is not the man of religion, but being utterly man, having only this one life in which to come to his self-realization, being utterly creature then, goes into the extremity of the truth of his Self, being God the Father, Creator, the Real, realized in this one moment, this one time, which He finds to be without surety. For, unless the man cries out of an utter and real destitution, deserted by reality, by truth, by the promise of the very Law he comes so far to fulfill, out of what that is not too trivial for the event does he cry—Why hast thou forsaken me?

We play in art, yes; and as artists show how much of the Father—even the ruthless mad old Father of the Old Testament—there is in Man as Maker, *homo faber*. But in every true poet's voice, in the full charm of the law or myth that moves us, you will hear also a counterpart of the Son's sorrow and pain of utter undergoing, the Passion, that the philosopher Plato thought the intelligence would modify and temper: the cross of the poem to the extent that it brings us into the fullness of its form or reality, brings us into the full condition of our living bodies, our utter individuality, our utter humanity. And third, we speak too as poets and must receive inspiration, the breath of Poetry where alone the Word passes from the immortality of its being written to the perishable sounding. Here, in what all men wonder at and least consider is the heart of poetry, the mere spirit from which the shapes of the vowels and consonants in their syllables are made, rime and measures, and the world of melody in which meanings, images and stories dance, is our little imitation of the Holy Ghost. The sounding is the love that moves the poet in language.

No person of that Identity upon the Cross, nor Creator nor Creature nor the Creation could have known the truth of that Identity—this is essential in the myth of the Passion; but, lost in the profound play of possibilities and impossibilities, God died from and into all the extensions of Its Self, so that the

Resurrection and Revelation is a new Identity of all persons and intentions. "If you have not entered the dance," the Christ says to John in the gnostic Gospel of John at Ephesus: "you misunderstand the event." But this *dance* is exactly the extremity out of which the ultimate cry of anguish comes. Each child, taking breath, leaps into life with such an anguish. At the heart of the Universe, the cosmic order that is a music in which the harmony of all things is established, in the fiat that it is Good, we remember there is also just this risk, this leaping into life or dying into life, that only mortal things know. So, the poet understands the truth of the anguish of Christ's passion as a truth of poetic form. The fullness of the creative imagination demands that rigor and painful knowledge be the condition of harmony; that death be the condition of eternal forms.

Yes, I care deeply and yet
you see in me how just
    where I should take care   I find
two sticks, a stone, and the wing
    of an ephemeral thing
——make it an orange butterfly with an eye
    of turquoise staring
even as I stare, lost in setting four
    factors of something I am making
        into motion.   Here
upon the threshold of salvation

I hold back, lingering, fashioning . . .
I am distracted from what I am.
Did you hear what I said, Robert?
    You are not paying attention . . .
and now I am
    making up, making my way
out of myself into the depths of my self;

for these are inanimate things, you would
     remind me; are yet
animate with my humanity I would
     not otherwise come to.

What soul have I, but the shape
of this one   life time,   patterns
     lost and patterns kept,
of two sticks and a stone, the fluttering
wing. Of dreams, yes. This angel
     likeness takes over color and
flight my mind knows to inhabit
     me. The whole wonderful heaven the stars
lead into

two sticks, a stone

     sleeps and dreams and is, the Hindoos
say, great Brahma, or Krishna,
     radiant desire dancing, and the stone

is at once a dead thing, a weight; and alive,
     from whose core a light
flashes or glows,

but if I wake, I will wake deeply
into the suffering of Man where that stone, the Heart,
is heavy, and climb

upon two sticks toward the center I am,
     a-light, thrown down from my wings into Love,
a stone, cry out   .   falling

     for His sake.

It was not a simple thing   I could not
explain then   these were most
     what they were   two sticks,
a stone, a colord wing
     invaded me. And when I go back to it,

[77]

when they come back to me,   pain
   gleams in the depths of that
extremity,   my rapture;   for the making up
   of every world lies in the seed
of two sticks and speaks from a little stone   .

   the soul   .   recognizes wings
as flight long known   the color
   itself a universe   so near
only my hands counting   and eyes
   naming these things

holds at bay   what is   from me.